ARTIFIC INTELLIGENCE AND GENERATIVE AI FOR BEGINNERS

An easy guide to learning about the world of AI and AI Generatives such as ChatGPT, Dall-E, Jasper, Midjourney, and much more

By Michael Gordon Cohen

Contents

What is an AI 5
   History of Artificial Intelligence 5
      How and When Was Artificial Intelligence Born? 6
      The History of Artificial Intelligence: From the Neural Networks of The 1950s to Today 7
   Types of Artificial Intelligence 10
   How Artificial Intelligence Works 12
   Examples of Artificial Intelligence 12
AI Techniques and How to Understand It 15
      Machine Learning 16
      Deep Learning and Neural Networks 17
      NLP – Natural Language Processing (Recognition and Processing of Natural Language) 18
      Computer Vision and Image Recognition 19
Concept of Generative AI 21
   What is Generative AI 21
   Advantages and Disadvantages of Generative Artificial Intelligence 22
   Benefits of Generative AI 23
   Disadvantages of Generative AI 23
   Technologies and uses of Generative AI 24
   What Are the Applications of Generative AI? 25
   How Generative AI Works 27
   What challenges do Generative AI and large language models face? 28
   What Will Be the Impact of AI Generative Models on Finance 30
   Popular Generative AI Applications 31

The Best Generative AI Tools 33
What Are the Secondary or Tertiary Ways That Generative Ai Will Manifest Itself In Our Lives? 35
Can Generative Ai Increase Productivity? 35
The Growth of Generative AI and Its Legal Issues 36
    AI-Generated Works Intellectual Property Rights: Who Owns the Rights to AI-Generated Works? 36
    AI Systems Accountability: Who is responsible when AI-generated decisions are wrong? 37
    Transparency in AI Systems and How to Limit Potential Biases In AI Models? 38
    Privacy and Cybersecurity Issues of Generative AI: How to Protect Individuals? 39
    Ethical Principles of an AI System 40
Different Generative AI 42
    Text to Text 42
    Text to Image 45
    Text to the video 48
    Text to Audio 50
    Audio to Text 53
        How These Audio-To-Text AI Tools Work 65
Field of Work Where Ai Could Be Beneficial 66
    Marketing and Advertising 66
    Finance and Accounting 77
    Healthcare 80
    Manufacturing and Logistics 84
    Customer Service 92
    Transportation 103

- Security 108
- Human Resources 109
- Legal Services 113
- Education and School 118
- Professional sports coaching 122
- Retail 127

Conclusion: The Future of AI and Generative AI 129

What is an AI

By developing methods that enable it to display intellectual activity, the field of artificial intelligence in computer science aims to build robots that mimic human intelligence. Artificial intelligence (AI) is a machine's ability of a device to mimic human qualities such as logic, learning, planning, and imagination.

Artificial intelligence enables systems to comprehend their surroundings, relate to what they observe, solve issues, and behave in a specific direction. The computer gets the information (prepared or received by sensors such as a video camera), processes it, and replies.

The technological maturity can explain the current ferment around this discipline achieved both in the computational calculation (today there are compelling hardware systems, small and with low energy consumption) and in the ability to analyze in real-time and in a short time vast amounts of data and any form (Analytics).

History of Artificial Intelligence

When we speak about Artificial Intelligence, we think of cutting-edge technologies, robots capable of understanding and selecting what actions to take, and a futuristic society where machines and humans coexist. Actuality, artificial intelligence, and their applications are far more accurate than one may assume. They are now used in various areas of daily life. However, these are less invasive uses than one thinks or what is often shown by science fiction films that have found the theme of Artificial Intelligence the starting point for mAs defined today any more or less successful series.

How and When Was Artificial Intelligence Born?

With the debut of computers in 1956, artificial intelligence as we know it today was born. This year, for the first time, Artificial Intelligence was briefly argued at an American conference, where the name was eventually recognized as Artificial Intelligence. Still, it was time for Intelligent systems. During this historic conference, some programs already capable of conducting logical reasoning, especially those related to mathematics, were presented. The Logic Theorist program, developed by Allen Newell and Herbert Simonf, could demonstrate theorems based on specific inputs.

The years after the conception of Artificial Intelligence were filled with great conceptual and experimental tumult: academic institutions and IT companies, particularly IBM, focused on researching and developing new programs and software which could think and act like humans, at least in specific fields and sectors. This is how programs capable of proving increasingly complex theorems were born. Above all, Lisp was born, the first programming language that, for over thirty years, was the basis of Artificial Intelligence software.

The uniqueness of the 1950s and 1960s was, above all, the sense of optimism that underpinned all studies and trials in this field: nevertheless, if, on the one hand, it was possible to develop ever more sophisticated software capable of solving above all mathematical calculations, from On the other hand, the first limitations of Artificial Intelligence began to be seen, which did not seem to be able to reproduce the intuitive and reasoning abilities typical of human beings.

During the second half of the sixties, it became increasingly evident that what had been achieved up to then in the field of Artificial Intelligence was no longer sufficient for the new needs, which were, above all, those of creating machines and programs capable of going beyond the 'simple' solution of more or less complex mathematical theorems. Instead, the new trend sought solutions to problems closer to human reality, such as the solution to issues whose answers could vary according to the evolution of the parameters during construction.

One of the significant challenges of the time was trying to reproduce software and machines that could reason and take solutions based on analyzing different possibilities. But this type of problem needed, before being solved, the resolution of another step: creating semantic paths for the machines, i.e., a language that would allow programming the different possibilities envisaged by reasoning, whether simple or complex. As often happens with significant discoveries and research, the passage from one step to another proved to be anything but simple: research in this sector suffered a sudden slowdown, above all because, due to the production of results, all funding for this type of research was drastically reduced.

The History of Artificial Intelligence: From the Neural Networks of The 1950s to Today

The scientific community's interest in artificial intelligence began a long time ago: the first precise artificial intelligence proposal (now referred to as AI) dates back to 1943, when two scientists Warren McCulloch, and Walter Pitt, introduced to the scientific world the first artificial neuron, which was followed in 1949by the book by Donby the Hebb, a Canadian psychologist, which established the links between artificial neurons and complex models of the human brain.

At the end of the 1950s, the first working models of neural networks (mathematical/computer models made to mimic the way biological neurons work to solve artificial intelligence problems, which in those days meant the ability of a machine to do things and think like a human mind) came out, and public. Public thanks to the young Alan Turing, who was already trying to explain how a computer could behave like a human mind in 1950.

The term artificial intelligence started "officially" by the American mathematician John McCarthy (in 1956) and, with it, the "launch" of the first programming languages (Lisp in 1958 and Prolog in 1973) specific for AI. From then on, the history of artificial intelligence was quite fluctuating, characterized by significant advances from the point of view of mathematical models (increasingly sophisticated models to "imitate" some brain functions such as pattern recognition) but with ups and downs from the point of view of research on hardware and neural networks.

The first central turning point on this latter front came in the 90s with the entry into the "enlarged" market (that is, reaching the general public) of graphics processors, the GPUs - graphics processing units (data processing chips much faster than CPUs, coming from the world of gaming and able to support complex processes much more quickly, moreover operating at lower frequencies and consuming less energy than the "old" CPUs).

The most recent wave has arrived in the last decade with the development of the so-called "neuromorphic chips," i.e., microchips that integrate data processing and storage in a single micro component (thanks to the acceleration that research in the field of nanotechnologies has also had) to emulate the sensory and cognitive functions of the human brain (the latter area where many startups are also focusing).

Looking a little at history, the first neural network model dates back to the end of the 1950s: it was the so-called "perceptron," proposed in 1958 by Frank Rosenblatt (known American psychologist and computer scientist), a network with an input layer and an output layer and an intermediate learning rule based on the error back-propagation algorithm (error minimization); the mathematical function, essentially, based on the evaluation of the adequate output data – concerning a given input – alters the weights of the connections (synapses) causing a difference between the productive output and the desired one.

Some industry experts trace the birth of cybernetics and artificial intelligence back to the Rosenblatt perceptron, even if, in the years immediately following, the two mathematicians Marvin Minsky and Seymour Paper demonstrated the limits of Rosenblatt's neural network model: the perceptron was able to recognize, after appropriate "training" only linearly separable functions (through the training set - the learning algorithm – in the vector space of the inputs, it is possible to separate those which require a positive output from those which need a negative output); furthermore, the computational capabilities of a single perceptron were limited, and performance strongly depended both on the choice of inputs and on the choice of algorithms through which to 'modify' the synapses and therefore the outputs.

The two mathematicians, Minsky and Papert, sensed that building a multi-level perceptron network could solve more complex problems. Still, in those years, the growing computational complexity required by training networks using algorithms needed to find an answer on an infrastructural level (not that there were hardware systems able to 'handle' such operations).

The first important turning point from a technological point of view came between the end of the 70s and the decade of the 80s with the development of the GPUs, which considerably reduced the training times of the networks, lowering them by 10/20 times.

Types of Artificial Intelligence

It is clear from this brief "historical voyage" that it is challenging to define artificial intelligence precisely. Nevertheless, we may pinpoint its general outlines and create some fundamental classifications by examining its development.

Weak and Strong Artificial Intelligence: What They Are and How They Differ

Although the impetus for artificial intelligence research started from the desire to imitate human intelligence, two distinct approaches and application strands have developed, albeit starting from standard assumptions. This is the case between weak artificial intelligence (or narrow AI) and vital artificial intelligence (or general AI).

To grasp the differences between strong AI and weak AI, a quick premise is appropriate, relating to the functions of human intelligence that artificial intelligence should be able to perform, in particular:

- ◊ Act humanely, in analogy with what a human being would do in the same situation
- ◊ Think humanly, solving a problem with cognitive functions
- ◊ Reason in a logical way, as man does in his reasoning
- ◊ Act rationally to try to get the best possible result based on the information available

This variety describes how imitating man is not a univocal operation but can be declined towards various approaches, which are precisely those that give rise to the research and application lines of weak AI and strong AI, as well as making us understand why the first is by now widely diffused. In contrast, the second constitutes a much more challenging objective to achieve.

Weak (weak AI)

Weak (or restricted) artificial intelligence refers to systems designed to solve specific problems of varying complexity. Its paradigm is problem-solving, as some resolution capacities of human cognition are simulated without, however, having the pretension to understand and replicate the functioning of everything the human brain can do.

Weak AI-based applications rely on machine learning to create systems capable of autonomously simulating scenarios and assisting human decisions in specific operations.

Whether figuring out how many goods to order in a supermarket, rather than planning the maintenance of a system or suggesting a purchase on an e-commerce portal, the goal is always to answer a practical need in the best possible way. Possible way, which only sometimes coincides with what the man would have done in the same situation.

Strong (strong AI)

Strong (or general) artificial intelligence refers to systems capable of behaving completely autonomously regardless of the context and the task assigned. This approach radically differs from the one envisaged for weak AI, as there is no direct link between the problem and the solution.

Problem-solving is not the crux of the matter, but developing an autonomous conscience that does not claim from time to time to emulate thought processes similar to those of man, aiming instead at developing a general intelligence, free from specific needs, and therefore effective in any situation.

If weak AI aims to act rationally and think humanely, strong AI focuses on working humanely and reasoning. For example, if weak AI has a problem, it tries to predict the man's choice rationally in that context. At the same time, strong AI is based on logical reasoning and uses the data available to generate knowledge of the context from which they derive the actions to be taken.

Weak AI acts on a case-by-case basis, solving only the resulting problem. Strong AI works, in general terms, starting from the game's rules, to solve all the issues that arise.

Another reference AI Lab is OpenAI (Microsoft), known for having developed GPT-3 (Generative Pre-Trained Transformer 3), a language model based on artificial intelligence capable of processing texts and images formally indistinguishable from what a human would do.

How Artificial Intelligence Works

We have observed how artificial intelligence (AI) technology functions. From the perspective of intellectual capabilities, an AI's operation is primarily supported by four distinct functional levels:

◊ **Understanding:** Artificial intelligence (AI) can detect words, photos, tables, videos, and voices and derive information from them via simulating cognitive data and event correlation capabilities.
◊ **Reasoning:** Through automated and exact mathematical methods, the systems can connect the various data obtained through logic.
◊ **Learning:** In this instance, we are referring to systems with particular capabilities for processing data inputs and ensuring their "proper" return in output (this is a classic illustration of machine learning systems, which use machine learning techniques to enable AI to learn and carry out diverse tasks).
◊ **Interaction (Human Machine Interaction):** We're discussing how AI engages with people. Natural Language Processing (NLP) systems, which use natural language to enable human-machine interaction (and vice versa), are making considerable progress in this area.

Examples of Artificial Intelligence

The Top companies such as Facebook, Google, Amazon, Apple, and Microsoft are battling not only to bring in innovative startups in the AI field but also to start and feed research projects of which we are already seeing some fruits today (such as the recognition of images, faces, voice applications, linguistic translations, etc.).

Because of today's technological maturity, artificial intelligence has moved from the realm of study to everyday life. In the commercial world, the maturity (and accessibility) of technical solutions have introduced the promise of AI into many segments. As consumers, we have essential "tastes" owing to Google and Facebook. These are the hottest ones right now:

Sales

- ◊ The usage of expert systems, which are programs that fall under the category of artificial intelligence since they mimic the performance of an expert individual in a particular field of knowledge or activity, has already produced notable results when applied to the sales industry.
- ◊ The solutions that integrate expert systems internally allow users (even non-experts) to solve particularly complex problems for which the intervention of a talented human being in the specific sector, activity, or domain of knowledge where the problem occurs would necessarily be needed.
- ◊ Simply put, they are systems that allow people to find a solution to a problem without requiring an expert's intervention. Moreover, from a technological point of view, expert systems allow for the automatic implementation of inference procedures (i.e., logic: with an inductive or deductive process, one reaches a conclusion following the analysis of a series of facts or circumstances).

Marketing

- ◊ Vocal/virtual assistants (Microsoft's Cortana, Chatbots, Apple's Siri, and Amazon's Alexa) that use artificial intelligence for natural language identification as well as learning and analyzing user habits and behaviors; Large data sets are being studied in real-time for better to understand people's "sentiments" and needs. This will help to improve customer service, user experience, assistance, and support services. It will also help to develop and perfect sophisticated engagement mechanisms with activities that extend beyond the point of purchase.
- ◊ For some years now, AI in Marketing has been showing all its maximum power and most significant area of use with users.

Healthcare

- ◊ AI offers the benefit of enhancing several assistive technologies already used by individuals with disabilities (for instance, vocal systems have advanced to the point where they enable completely authentic relationships and communication even for those unable to talk). Still, it is at the front of the diagnosis and treatment of tumors and rare diseases that it will be possible to see the new capabilities of AI.
- ◊ Cognitive systems are already on the market and capable of drawing, analyzing, and learning from an infinite pool of data (scientific publications, research, medical records, data on drugs, etc.) at a rate that is unfathomable to a humans. As a result, these systems can speed up making crucial diagnoses for rare diseases or suggesting the best course of action for treating tumors or specific conditions.
- ◊ Additionally, AI-based virtual assistants are beginning to interact with one another more regularly in operating rooms, helping front-desk employees or those providing first aid.

Cybersecurity

- ◊ One of the more developed uses of artificial intelligence is fraud prevention, where the technology takes the form of highly complex analyses that correlate data, events, behaviors, and habits to anticipate any fraudulent activities (like copying a credit card or carrying out an unauthorized transaction); In actuality, these technologies can also be used in other organizational settings, such as risk reduction, information and data protection, and the fight against cybercrime.

Supply Chains

- ◊ The optimization and management of the supply and distribution chain now require sophisticated analyzes, and, in this case, AI is the effective system that allows you to connect and monitor the entire supply chain and all the players involved, a very significant case of application of artificial intelligence to the supply chain management sector is related to order management.

Public Security

- ◊ There is a great deal of potential for increasing the effectiveness and efficiency of public safety by using the ability to analyze massive amounts of data in real-time and "deduce" through correlations of occasions, routines, behaviors, attitudes, geo-location systems, and data as well as monitoring the movement of things and people.
- ◊ For instance, crisis management and prevention during natural catastrophes like earthquakes and tsunamis or security and crime prevention in airports, train stations, and major cities.

AI Techniques and How to Understand It

The distinction between weak and strong AI is fundamental for correctly connoting the central artificial intelligence techniques. As we were able to observe in the historical introduction, these are topics that began to be discussed between the 1950s and 1970s; even if it was necessary to wait many decades to have a significant diffusion, waiting for Moore's law took its course, eventually producing computational systems capable of providing the power required to perform the necessary calculations.

While waiting for Quantum Computing to become a reality also for commercial applications, the major technological leap derives from the market introduction of GPUs (Graphic Processing Units), processors initially conceived for graphic rendering, whose parallel computing nature is also pleasant to other application areas, including artificial intelligence systems and cryptocurrency mining.

Let's see a quick review of some of the current leading artificial intelligence techniques, starting with the substantial difference between Machine Learning and Deep Learning, particularly the learning models on which they are based.

Machine Learning

By Machine Learning, we mean an automatic learning system based on artificial intelligence, capable of acquiring a variety of data (input) to train a machine that becomes progressively more and more able to carry out a task (output) autonomously, i.e., without having been previously scheduled to run it, an ML system stands out for its ability to learn, make mistakes, and progressively improve from its mistakes until it becomes more and more precise in the simulations that it can produce in total autonomy.

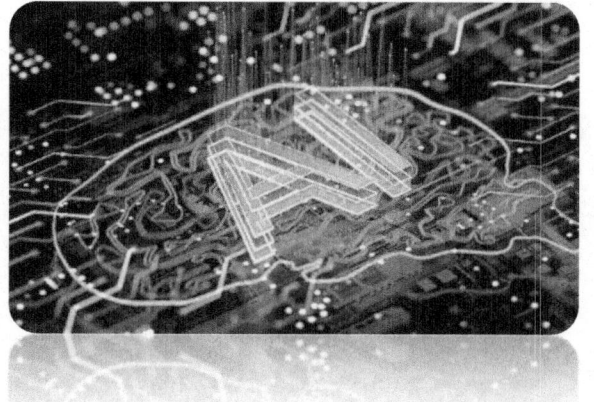

The learning model of an ML system is quite varied and is based on three main classes of algorithms:

◊ **With didactic supervision:** in which the system learns through a correlation between inputs and outputs, from which it learns how to make a decision

◊ **Without didactic supervision:** learning takes place through the analysis of the results, without a direct relationship between inputs and outputs, but dwelling only based on works that allow mapping the effects of certain decisions in the same context in which ML systems are called to offer solutions.

◊ **With reinforcement:** reinforcement learning is a learning method based on merit, as AI is rewarded only when it obtains a result that matches expectations in its evaluations.

Reinforcement learning allows you to refine the training of an ML system thanks to its ability to teach how to distinguish a correct decision from an incorrect one.

By examining its development, we may pinpoint its general outlines and create some fundamental classifications.

Deep Learning and Neural Networks

If Machine Learning is a typical tool of the so-called weak AI, Deep Learning is the reference learning technique for strong AI. In line with the previously described theoretical-conceptual premise, Deep Learning consists of learning models inspired by the functioning of the human brain.

It is not a training method strictly based on the relationship between an input and an output, as in the case of ML, but a system that uses the information to emulate the human brain's behavior.

This is not surprising if we consider how many computer techniques are openly inspired by the structure of some biological models that exist in nature. For example, how an algorithm replicates a cooperative mechanism, such as the flight of birds, is incredibly fascinating.

Neural networks are structured networks of artificial neurons that allow the implementation of complex actions typical of human cognition, such as seeing, speaking, hearing, and thinking. Computer science perfectly historicized these concepts since artificial neurons were theorized by McCulloch and Pitts in 1943, while neural networks by Rosenblatt in 1958.

Deep learning is based on the so-called deep neural networks, characterized by many layers of calculation based on an extremely high number of levels, such as requiring an enormous computational effort to obtain a scenario like the human brain's neural connections; however, largely still unknown.

Since much emphasis is placed on the evolution of computational capabilities to guarantee the output, adequate focus must also be paid to the moment of creation of the input, thanks to the ability to a massive amount of data from mobile devices and, in general, from all the interconnected devices with which we interact daily, even in a completely unconscious way, thanks to the ease with which we accept the use policies of the apps on the various devices.

An increasingly digitized reality translates into an enormous potential for data to be collected, archived, analyzed, and processed. Yet, data science has to be called upon to assume an essential role in applications based on artificial intelligence.

NLP – Natural Language Processing (Recognition and Processing of Natural Language)

Natural language processing represents a complex application based on AI, computer science, and linguistics. It is one of the most widespread expressions of the so-called strong AI, which it exemplifies perfectly, thanks to the fact that it is not conceived to solve a specific aspect but to learn human verbal communication in a broad sense, with which applications based on AI are calls to interact.

Understanding a language is decidedly complex because it's not just a question of knowing how to manage vocabulary, grammar, and syntax rules but of learning how to correctly contextualize a speech to understand the meaning of a statement.

The NLP learning method is based on Deep learning systems built to simulate how people understand a conversation's content. An NLP system is based on a series of steps that attempt to identify and resolve all ambiguities in human language. Phase separation is crucial to lowering the likelihood of input data errors. Among the main phases of an NLP learning method are tokenization, morphological and lexical analysis, syntactic analysis, NER (Named Entity Recognition), Semantic analysis, and discourse analysis.

Research on NLP has been active since the early 2000s. Still, it has been able to reach appreciable levels of maturity starting from 2013 when neural networks spread with the deepening of techniques relating to the representation of natural language in a numerical way, where each word is "converted" into a vector of real numbers managed by spatial vector models, neural network architectures specially designed to solve natural language recognition and processing.

NLP is now an integral part of many applications ranging from machine translation to automatic recognition (OCR), to chatbots/virtual assistants, to the automatic generation of complex texts for publications, and the tools used in marketing to analyze the so-called sentiment of users (sentiment analysis).

From the point of view of text understanding and processing, NLP systems are already surprisingly mature. However, at the same time, there is still a lot to do as regards the creation of intelligent systems capable of fully expressing the potential of general artificial intelligence.

We've seen a couple of science fiction movies movie thus far. Think of Her, where Joaquin Phoenix establishes a real sentimental relationship with a computer whose operating system is capable of perfectly understanding verbal communication, as well as expressing itself with the very sensual voice of Scarlett Johannson.

Computer Vision and Image Recognition

One of the fascinating aspects of computer vision is based on image recognition, i.e., the emulation of how the human brain processes information received from the eyes rather than on the watch's functioning.

Understanding what you are seeing is the objective. To achieve this result, learning methods capable of processing the individual pixels of an image, in other words, translating them into numbers, are needed.

Computer vision uses Deep Learning techniques based on convolutional neural networks, capable of emulating the behavior of the brain's visual cortex to process immense image datasets to precisely recognize and contextualize the image that is recognized in real-time by the 'application.

There are a great many examples based on computer vision. However, the most prevalent concern is facial recognition technologies many applications use, including the procedure for unlocking mobile devices rather than access authorization.

For instance, quality control in the industrial sector uses computer vision. In contrast, autonomous driving uses it, for example, to recognize signs, other vehicles, pedestrians, and all the potential obstacles a car may encounter along its route. There are also many B2C marketing applications in collaboration with augmented reality technologies.

Concept of Generative AI

Among the emerging applications of Artificial Intelligence (Gartner has included it among the technological trends of 2022, destined to drive the digital transformation business between now and 2024), Generative AI – or Generative Artificial Intelligence – can produce synthetic data and supporting the abilities and creative activities of human beings.

The technologies related to Generative AI include those that allow a machine learning system - suitably trained using themed datasets - to produce artificial content and synthetic data of various kinds.

The multimedia industry, healthcare, the world of art and design, and the production of new products represent the areas where generative AI applications are increasingly widespread.

What is Generative AI

Generative AI allows computers to kinds of new and exciting content for more than just t for fun; Generative AI has many practical uses, such as creating new product designs and optimizing business processes.

One of the newly developed uses for artificial intelligence is generative AI. Its productive capacity makes it possible to produce synthetic data and to support man in his creative activities. As a result, Generative AI applications are increasingly popular in the multimedia industry, healthcare, art, design, and the production of new products.

Generative AI is a research field that is also part of the broader field of artificial intelligence, which focuses on building AI systems that can either generate new data or create new versions of existing data. Algorithms that fall into this ambit include all those that make it possible to create highly realistic images of faces and those that generate more structured data or sounds, videos, etc. These results can be achieved through various methods, both deterministic and non-deterministic. Depending on your goal and quality, you must deal with machine learning, natural language processing (NLP), and digital image processing.

Advantages and Disadvantages of Generative Artificial Intelligence

Generative AI models can be helpful in many cases. For example, new data can be beneficial to increase the size of a dataset and use it to train other artificial intelligence systems since modern models can generate remarkably realistic data (i.e., similar and almost indistinguishable from real ones). Similarly, they can be used to create new versions of existing datasets so that they can be used to confirm other AI systems.

Furthermore, the latest applications suggest the use of these models also to support the generation of original content, including those that consist of images, videos, audio, or texts.

In the last period, however, generative artificial intelligence has begun to worry many people, especially those who deal with creative works, which would risk being replaced by algorithms. According to the most critical, these models could also be used for many subtler and more dangerous purposes, exploiting the inability of human beings to distinguish them from actual data, as happens, simple example, with deep fakes (extremely incredibly artificial videos, in which images of real people to create false but very plausible situations).

Benefits of Generative AI

Here are the benefits that Generative AI brings:

◊ **Higher Quality Outputs** – Generative AI can erase noise in images and videos, increasing overall output quality.
◊ **Cheaper Processes** – By dramatically reducing the time and cost involved in drug and material discovery in manufacturing, products can become cheaper.
◊ **Productivity Booster** – By reducing time and the amount of work, generative AI helping creative people can increase their productivity.
◊ **Improved Health** – Using adversarial generative networks (GANs) in early cancer detection means better health.
◊ **New Inventions** – Using neural networks to synthesize new chemicals, models, substances, or anything else can potentially lead to new inventions.

Disadvantages of Generative AI

There are also some issues with Generative AI, such as the limits of creativity, setup costs, and ethical considerations. Here's a closer look:

Limited Creativity – Although generative AI produces new things, no original thought is needed because the result is typically a composite of the input fed into the neural network. AI systems, in other terms, lack creativity. Since they depend on human input information to capsulize and create concepts, they cannot.

However, the 6th chakra functionality in the human energy system of yoga perfectly aligns with the pattern recognition function of machine learning and the creative components of generative AI. So we're safe as long as the machines stay that way; the chakras' abilities to understand and conceptualize information, those same characteristics that distinguish us from other animals so that humans may be on the verge of extinction.

High Setup Cost – The initial setup of AI systems can be increased, although this is expected to decrease in the future.

Moral and Ethical Considerations - From deep fakes depicting politicians and celebrities saying funny or bizarre things to controversial apps like deep-nude that have incited a backlash from feminists, there's no limit to the possible adverse outcomes of using generative AI.

Technologies and uses of Generative AI

Generative AI includes a variety of technologies that allow a machine learning system, suitably trained thanks to a set of thematic data sets, to create artificial content and synthetic data of various kinds.

The most representative technology of the fertile generative Artificial Intelligence field is GANs (Generative Adversarial Networks), mainly known for creating deep fakes, audio-video content capable of replacing the natural counterpart accurately. Among the most frequent examples, we have replaced the face in a video, perfectly coherent with its facial animation, or created fake audio with a voice identical to that of the subject to be imitated.

GANs aren't the only technology active in the Generative AI space. Among the most widespread, we also find transformers (e.g., GPT and LaMDA) highly effective with the language, and variation auto-encoders, are also available in various mobile apps.

Despite the young age of technology, the applications of Generative AI are already quite widespread. It is not uncommon to meet them, in addition to the aforementioned deep fakes, in contexts such as:

Image Processing: reconstruction of higher resolution images with a higher level of detail

Video Restoration on Analog Support: very popular for "remastering" old generation films, bringing them comfortably to 4K with 60fps, cleaning up the image, making it sharper, complete with a color reconstruction

Simulations in the medical field: in support of 3D technologies to pre-visualize prostheses and molecular organisms

Support diagnostic activity and microbiological research: the ability to detect malignant situations in early diagnosis and conduct research on pathogens

Protection of privacy: protection of sensitive identities through avatars to make it impossible to recognize people who could be victims of persecution, for example, when giving an interview

Furthermore, increasingly structured trends are beginning to emerge, capable of going well beyond the potential of a single application, increasingly taking shape as autonomous disciplines in the use of the generative capabilities of Artificial Intelligence

What Are the Applications of Generative AI?

Some ways that Generative AI can be used are:

- ◊ Generate new ideas
- ◊ Create products or services
- ◊ Design of new processes or systems
- ◊ Optimization of operations
- ◊ Discovery of new drugs or treatments

You can use Generative AI to improve your business in a few ways.

- ◊ First, it can be used to inspire fresh concepts. This can be accomplished by employing algorithms that mimic the process of natural selection and evolution.
- ◊ Secondly, generative AI can create new products or services. This can be accomplished by employing algorithms that mimic the human creative process.

- ◊ Third, generative AI can design new processes or systems. This can be accomplished by employing algorithms that mimic the human design process.
- ◊ Fourth, you can use generative AI to optimize your operations. This can be accomplished by employing algorithms that mimic the human optimization process.
- ◊ Fifth, one can use generative artificial intelligence to discover new drugs or treatments. This can be accomplished by employing algorithms that mimic the human discovery process.

How Generative AI Works

Artificial intelligence studies initially focused on using algorithms and neural networks to find patterns in large datasets. This has been used for pattern recognition, analysis, decision support, and anomaly detection.

Neural networks are digital representations of the human brain used to model the brain's natural system of thought. Such a network has input, and output layers of neurons, with one or more layers, called the hidden layer.

Input and Output Level Generate AI

Put the fire one input neuron for every data unit, such as a word. Therefore, the three input neurons for red, hot, and sun will activate when the term "hot sun" is given into a neural network, for instance. And on the output layer, let those three inputs know they mean "hot sun. "

After training such a network with "hot sun," "green hot sun," "cold green sun," and "yellow cold sun," it may initially appear foolish and time-consuming, but eventually, it will start to understand what spicy, green, and chilly could be.

Even though neural networks are difficult to understand, learning about them is a fascinating trip into consciousness, the human mind, and intellect.

Furthermore, neural network technology has evolved into new systems and platforms that enable today's generative AI applications. Here are 3 of the popular neural networks used:

Generative Adversarial Networks (GANs) – This neural network uses two parties to generate an output. The generator in the first half creates an unexpected result, and the discriminator in the second section assesses the work to determine if it is true or false.

GANs use an unsupervised learning system, meaning the discriminating part teaches the generator. Over time, the discriminator gets better at spotting fakes, and the generator improves at making images look more authentic.

Transformer – This is a different kind of neural network that can store any data sequence in a separate line, which a decoder can subsequently recreate.

Transformers work best for projects with sequential data, such as natural language sentences and music. Popular transformer-based neural networks include Microsoft's GPT-3, Wu Dao 2.0 from Beijing, China, and Google's LaMDA.

Automatic Variation Encoders (VAE) – This third kind of neural network is used to draw, scale, classify, and detect objects and noise in images. VAE models use an unsupervised learning method to shrink data files using compression algorithms and models.

What challenges do Generative AI and large language models face?

Before generative AI realizes its full potential, several obstacles must be overcome. The complexity of the data presents one of the most significant difficulties.

Generative AI requires access to large volumes of data to generate meaningful results, which can be difficult for some companies to obtain. Therefore, companies must ensure they have enough data to create significant effects. In addition, generative AI must be trained frequently to stay up with emerging trends and technology.

Generative AI can also have accuracy issues, as it can be difficult for these models to distinguish between actual and generated data. Therefore, businesses must be cautious about employing reputable sources. I recommend you evaluate Japser.ai or CHATGPT. Jasper.ai is a text-based AI platform developed by InvestGlass. It uses advanced linguistic processing and rule-based logic to generate automated conversation scripts that drive sales conversations through the InvestGlass CRM.

CHATGPT with OpenAI

CHATGPT is a chatbot platform based on deep learning and is also used to drive automated conversations. These platforms are based on extensive training datasets such as GPT three and Stabel Diffusion. Some models use CLIP (Contrastive Language-Image Pre-training) and diffusion models. Diffusion models are transformer-based generative models. They produce realistic photographs from textual descriptions of simple objects such as birds and cars. Some models can also be hosted on-premises to avoid queries outside your environment.

Contact relationship within InvestGlass

Generative AI faces a challenge that could be the price move. Given how simp, we may pinpoint its general outlines and create some fundamental classifications by examining its development to gauge how much a security's price might decline.

No computing power is needed to produce text or generate realistic images. This is the next ten years' greatest threat - or opportunity. The intelligence of this algorithm generates authentic photos that are not fake. They are photo-realistic images built with an intelligent generative model. It's about computer vision.

What Will Be the Impact of AI Generative Models on Finance

Generative AI models are increasingly used in finance to improve operations and increase profits. For example, sentiment analysis is one application that enables financial institutions to understand better customer sentiment and their reactions to products or services. Using this technology, financial institutions can make informed decisions about how to market their products, manage customer service, and optimize sales strategies.

Furthermore, Generative AI models can also be used in risk management and fraud detection. Thanks to technology, financial institutions can detect suspicious activity more quickly and precisely.

Additionally, Generative AI models can create detailed customer profiles that can be used to tailor financial services to each customer. As a result, banks can offer customers the products and services that best suit their needs.

Collectively, generative AI models have the potential to revolutionize the financial industry. This technology can help banks make more intelligent decisions that will benefit customers in the long run by improving operations, increasing profits, and tailoring financial services to each customer. So, it's an exciting time for finance as we integrate this technology into InvestGlass tools.

What Effects Will Generative AI Have on Society?

Shortly, Generative AI will replace most banking and consulting drafting duties. Technology will be deeply integrated into the value creation of InvestGlass. This will change business models and social media posts; bankers will jump on new buzzwords and make sure their faces are real human faces. Delivering genuinely creative work will be more challenging as the unsupervised generated model will be finished. Customers will also be equipped with a deep fake technology algorithm to check whether what they are looking at is real.

The first training set will be coded with InvestGlass' advisory module, but the next word will be generated by AI, starting with existing data and a natural language model layer. The model is built without causing code and does not need large models. The first drafts are adapted with the InvestGlass team and with your bankers/sellers, then the generative AI tools produce new content. This will be the most efficient way to write new buzzwords and refine solicitations. If your salespeople or bankers want to write original content, they can manually erase and write over existing text.

Generative AI models are becoming increasingly popular in the finance industry to improve operations, increase profits and provide clients with personalized services. InvestGlass leads the way with its AI solutions for sales and CRM, set to revolutionize the financial sector.

Popular Generative AI Applications

Generative AI technology can be applied in many industries requiring human creativity. The following is a look at its most popular applications and industries.

- ◊ **Images** – The generation of all-new AI graphics, using a text-to-image creation system or automatically modifying images, such as adding facial features, glasses, etc. The unpopular nudist app has gone as far as to undress people automatically.

- ◊ **Video** – Generative AI is also employed in video creation, such as turning a person's image into a talking video, making the famous Mona Lisa smile painting, and talking digital avatars that look and sound like real people.
- ◊ **Text** – This includes written text and computer code using natural language processing (NLP). The domain is vast, from chatbots to grammar checkers and writing assistants for copywriters and programmers.
- ◊ **Hollywood Movies** – Beyond only making videos, generative AI can be used in even more imaginative contexts, such as employing deep fakery to entirely alter the appearance of an actor, changing their agenda, inventing unique characters like the Marvel warlord Thanos, and even producing scripts and storylines on its own.
- ◊ **Music** – Generative AI is equally set to disrupt the music industry from gaming neural networks to the more complex systems that compose music in a wide variety of semi-assisted or fully automated genres.
- ◊ **Healthcare** – A range of applications, including augmentation of body scans to provide better information for diagnosis.
- ◊ **Fashion** – From diverse styles to personalized custom outfits, colors, trend predictions, and textures, generative AI is equally poised to disrupt the fashion industry.
- ◊ **E-commerce Personalization** – Techniques used to predict a customer's preferences and even move forward to offer proactive solutions, experiences, targeted communications, personalized product recommendations, etc.
- ◊ **Data Augmentation** – Creating new data points from existing but limited data to increase available information.
- ◊ **Manufacturing** – Generative AI aids in synthesizing new materials, chemicals, and drugs that can reduce manufacturing costs.

Project Ideas for Generative AI

It's frequently best to learn by doing. So, if you're interested in generative AI and its possibilities, there's no better way to try it than with a test project. Here are some suggestions to get you going:

- Produce non-existent faces.
- Facial aging or manipulation app.
- Create new human poses from images.
- Produce higher image resolutions.
- Colorize black and white images.
- Create 3D objects from 2D images.
- Create cartoon characters.
- Remove noise from images.
- NLP intention classification chat system.
- Short summaries of lengthy articles.
- Text-to-image artwork creations.
- CT scan detection to improve cancer diagnosis.

The Best Generative AI Tools

Many people and organizations have developed various tools that can help you with your Generative AI project in one way or another. Below are some of the most popular of these tools:

- **OpenAI** – Natural Language Processing GPT-3 and the natural language for code translation of Codex templates.
- **GAN Lab** – Generative Adversarial Network in your browser.
- **NightCaffè** – AI art generator.
- **TorchGan** – GAN training framework using Pytorch.
- **Pigano** – Python library for implementing GAN.
- **TF-GAN** – Tensorflow lightweight tools for GAN.
- **Google Cloud AI** – Collection of artificial intelligence tools from Google.
- **AI Duet** – Thanks to this, you may perform a piano duet with your computer.
- **Art Breeder** – Remix images to create unique works of art.

- ◊ **T5 Code** – Transformer-based model for understanding and generating code.
- ◊ **AI Camouflage** – Copy and imitate anyone's voice.
- ◊ **GAN Toolkit** – No-code GAN model framework.
- ◊ **HyperGAN** – Compassable Python framework with UI and API.
- ◊ **Deep Dream** – Computer vision program.
- ◊ **Imaginary** – PyTorch deep imaging library from Nvidia.
- ◊ **Cartoonize** – Create cartoon-like images.
- ◊ **TensorFlow** – Popular machine learning platform.
- ◊ **Scikit-learn** – Another machine learning platform in Python.
- ◊ **SLAB** – Impressive text to image creator.

What Are the Secondary or Tertiary Ways That Generative Ai Will Manifest Itself In Our Lives?

Unsurprisingly, many of the first uses of generative AI were by large tech companies or digital natives. However, generative AI will permeate the manufacturing, healthcare, and pharmaceutical sectors in the coming years. A generic addition, the active model can be tailored for content domains with significantly less input once trained.

We see specialized generative models for biomedical content, legal documents, and translated texts, giving rise to different use cases in these industries and domains. For example, they could help organizations manage their knowledge and content more effectively so that it is easily accessible to employees and customers.

Can Generative Ai Increase Productivity?

McKinsey & Company says that generative AI and other foundational models are changing the AI game, bringing assistive technology to a new level, shortening the time it takes to make an app, and giving powerful features to people who need to be tech-savvy.

Generative AI could improve efficiency and productivity, cut costs, and create new growth opportunities by making it possible to automate many tasks that used to be done by humans. For this reason, companies able to effectively exploit this technology will obtain a significant competitive advantage.

Although the software is still in progress, it takes little to realize generative AI's power. And millions are trying every day: to date, OpenAI servers can barely keep up with demand, so much so that a message regularly appears inviting users to come back later when the server's capacity is low.

The Growth of Generative AI and Its Legal Issues

GPT-3 exploits the so-called generative artificial intelligence (AI), also known as Generative Adversarial Networks (GANs), a type of artificial intelligence capable of generating new content, such as images, videos, and texts, without human intervention. It does this by training on a large set of examples and learning to create new examples that are similar and different from the ones seen previously. It may be used in any industry to provide content and boost business performance in various sectors, including healthcare, finance, and industrial and manufacturing. Synthetic data can also train other AI models and raise their effectiveness.

Several legal issues need to be addressed, from the intellectual property rights of AI-generated works to the liability of generative AI. But these challenges are accompanied by a series of possibilities with a revolution in business operations and improved efficiency. Therefore, it is essential to find a balance between taking advantage of the potential of generative AI and solving the legal problems that come with it.

AI-Generated Works Intellectual Property Rights: Who Owns the Rights to AI-Generated Works?

One of the crucial legal issues of generative AI concerns the ownership of intellectual property rights. The ability of AI systems to create new works without human intervention raises questions about who owns the rights to these works and how to protect them from infringement. Some argue that AI-generated results should be considered "orphan works" and not subject to copyright protection, as the creator cannot be identified. Similarly, in some litigation, it has been established that an AI cannot be the inventor under patent law.

This scenario raises concern for more about the lack of protection of these works and their potential for misuse. To address this problem, one possible solution is to create a new category of intellectual property rights specifically for AI-generated works. But this would make an extra layer of intellectual property rights that must be attributed to someone and could limit the exploitation of artificial intelligence.

The same goes for synthetic data, artificially generated by AI systems rather than gathered from natural sources. For example, if an AI system generates synthetic images based on authentic images, who owns the rights to the synthetic images? The rights of the original data creators and the rights of the creators of the synthetic data are called into doubt by this. And there is already a heated debate over the subject.

AI Systems Accountability: Who is responsible when AI-generated decisions are wrong?

As AI systems become more advanced, they will exponentially make decisions that can have significant consequences, such as diagnosing medical conditions, approving loans, and even driving our vehicles. There are some regulatory restrictions, and, for example, in the healthcare sector, an AI system is not licensed to provide medical treatment and, therefore, can only support doctors. Similarly, the highway code is designed to ensure that drivers are always in control of their vehicles, even if some incidents in recent years show that someone is abusing the potential of self-driving cars.

Additionally, under privacy laws, people have the right to be free from automated decision-making and, in any case, to request that a human review such decisions. This right has been strengthened in Italy by the so-called Transparency Decree regarding systems that monitor employees.

In case of errors due to errors in the AI system, questions arise as to who is responsible for them. Some argue that the creators of the AI system should be held accountable, while others suggest that it should be held liable.

An accountability regime for artificial intelligence is essential to foster its exploitation. Consequently, the European Commission is addressing the issue with a proposal for an EU directive. The question is whether such proposals strike the right balance between holding companies accountable for errors caused by AI and avoiding onerous obligations that could hinder the growth of AI.

Transparency in AI Systems and How to Limit Potential Biases In AI Models?

As generative AI systems become more complex, they become more challenging to understand and explain, making it difficult to determine why a particular decision was made. This can make it difficult to hold someone accountable for mistakes. Similarly, AI models could incorporate a prejudice (the so-called "bias") which could lead to unfair treatment of certain groups/categories of individuals. This might occur, for instance, if the AI system makes decisions that are biased against particular people or groups due to partial data that was used to train the AI model.

Biases in generative AI can lead to legal and ethical problems due to the potential risk of discrimination.

The European Commission is trying to address this aspect of artificial intelligence with the AI law which has now been adopted by the European Council and which is expected to introduce different levels of certification and regimes for various types of AI, depending on the potential risks resulting from it (Read "The EU Council adopts the AI Act proposal on artificial intelligence ").

There currently needs to be a comprehensive federal law explicitly addressing AI in the United States. However, several rules and regulations apply to various aspects of AI.

- Privacy: The California Consumer Privacy Act (CCPA) and the Children's Online Privacy Protection Act (COPPA), which govern how businesses gather and handle personal data, were both impacted by the General Data Protection Regulation (GDPR) in Europe. Guidelines for data security and privacy are also applicable to AI and are provided by the Federal Trade Commission (FTC).
- Employment: However, employment regulations like the Fair Labor Standards Act (FLSA) and the Americans with Disabilities Act (ADA) still apply to employees whether or not AI is replacing them, even though no particular laws limit the use of AI in the workplace.
- Intellectual Property: The Patent and Trademark Office (USPTO) has issued guidelines on patenting AI inventions, and copyright laws apply to AI-generated works as they do to human-generated results.
- Discrimination: AI decision-making is subject to discrimination regulations, including the Civil Rights Act and the Age Discrimination in Employment Act. However, there is concern that AI may perpetuate biases in data and algorithms, leading to unintentional discrimination.
- Autonomous Vehicles: The National Highway Traffic Safety Administration has revealed requirements for testing and deploying autonomous vehicles, and some states have their own rules.

Privacy and Cybersecurity Issues of Generative AI: How to Protect Individuals?

With the ability of AI systems to generate realistic images and videos, there are concerns that this technology could be used to invade people's privacy and safety. Further raising doubts about the veracity of information and the media is the use of generative AI in "deep fake content," which may be used to produce phony films and photos.

AI in deep fake content can be used to create fake videos and images, which can spread disinformation or harass or blackmail people. This technology can also create realistic photos of people, which can be used for malicious purposes such as catfishing and identity theft. Additionally, the use of generative AI in creating synthetic data for use in training other AI models raises concerns about the privacy of people who may be represented in the data.

A further concern is that generative AI systems can be used to identify bugs in code that facilitate potential cyberattacks, including ransomware attacks. Similarly, generative AA can reproduce the voice and image of CEOs and high-level executives to conduct so-called "Fake CEO" cyber-attacks.

Ethical Principles of an AI System

To respond to this need, the European Commission has released a contribution, "Ethical Guidelines for reliable AI," which addresses possible contraindications in developing AI systems.

Four ethical principles have been identified, rooted in fundamental human rights, which must be adhered to ensure that AI systems are developed, distributed, and used reliably.

Humans with AI systems must maintain their complete and adequate self-determination to respect their autonomy. AI systems must, therefore, not subordinate, coerce, deceive, manipulate, condition, or unjustifiably aggregate human beings' damage prevention means that AI systems must not cause damage or aggravate it or even negatively affect human beings, for whom it is necessary to protect human dignity and physical and mental integrity. AI systems and the environments in which they operate must be safe and secure. They must be technically robust, and it must be ensured that they are not exposed to malicious use.

Equity: which implies a commitment to ensure a fair and equitable distribution of costs and benefits; that the use of AI systems must never deceive users or hinder their freedom of choice; that AI industry players respect the principle of proportionality between means and ends, and carefully consider how to balance competing interests and goals

Explicability: implying that processes governed by AI must be transparent.

An AI system's potential and purpose must be made clear, and actions must, to the extent possible, be explicable to people they may directly or indirectly impact. Therefore, starting from these principles, to obtain reliable AI systems, three central components have been identified, which have been developed into seven requirements which are declined into a series of sub-requirements that aim to put into practice these requirements throughout the lifecycle of an AI-powered system. These components are:

- ◊ Legality, the AI must comply with all applicable laws and regulations.
- ◊ Ethics, AI must ensure adherence to ethical principles and values
- ◊ Robustness, from a technical and social point of view to the AI , causing unintentional damage.

Each component is necessary, but more is needed to build trustworthy AI. Ideally, the three parts should work harmoniously and be superimposable.

Different Generative AI

Generative Artificial Intelligence refers to machine learning and deep learning techniques to generate new content based on previous data. In particular, we are talking about using large language models (Large Language Models), which allow us to obtain texts, images, videos, and unpublished code starting from textual input.

Text to Text

The most advanced field is creating texts from text input. The models can generate excellent short and medium-length texts, already used in practical applications of copywriting and automatic writing of newspaper articles. In the next few years, we will have better first drafts than professional one's writing: the "text to text" linguistic models have given rise to many tools that can be used in marketing and sales for the rapid creation of texts for commercial emails, newsletters, and social media posts.

- ◊ Writing: software to assist in the correct drafting of texts. For now, they are generalists, but a "virtualization" of the same is foreseen to cover more specific topics, such as the writing of legal texts or film scripts.
- ◊ Intelligent assistants: in this case, the models aim to make chat conversations more believable and valuable.
- ◊ Knowledge: artificial intelligence is used here to improve the search for information in the company (Glean) or on the web (You) and to self-organize the workspace (Mem).

1. Jasper AI

Jasper is a neural network-based AI text generator that can produce material that resembles that of a human. One of the most sophisticated AI text generators currently accessible, it is based mainly on GPT-3 and was developed by OpenAI, an artificial intelligence of many centers.

Jasper needs many training data to create high-quality results, yet its output frequently has to be more different from that of a human writer. Jasper is also incredibly adaptable and can be used to create various materials, such as articles, blog entries, product descriptions, and more.

For instance, I generated the first 500 words of this essay using Jasper's "One Shot Blog Post" template. Additionally, Jasper includes a direct interface with Surfer SEO, allowing you to use all the suggested keywords and resources to raise the search engine ranking of your blogs.

My go-to AI copywriting tool is Jasper, especially for lengthy articles. They continuously test several language models using their text and AI picture generators to find the best consumer results.

Price: Basic plans begin at $24 per month, but their Boss Mode plan, which starts at $49 per month when paid annually, is the best value.

2. Frase

Frase.io is a content optimization platform that uses AI to help businesses improve their website content. The platform offers tools to help companies to create, optimize, and distribute more compelling content to drive traffic, engagement, and conversions.

The AI-powered tools offered by Frase.io include the following:

- Content Briefs: Frase.io uses AI to analyze top-ranking content in a particular topic area and provides a detailed brief on the key topics and subtopics that should be covered in a new piece of content.
- Answer Engine Optimization (AEO): Frase.io's AEO tool uses AI to help businesses optimize their content to answer better specific questions that users might have. This can drive more traffic and improve engagement on a website.

- Content Optimization: Frase.io's AI-powered content optimization tool can analyze existing content and suggest changes to improve its effectiveness, such as adding more keywords, improving readability, or adding multimedia.
- Content Distribution: Frase.io's AI can also help businesses distribute their content more effectively by identifying the best channels and timing for sharing it.

3. Copysmith

An AI text generator called Copysmith is focused on producing marketing copy. It has many tools, such as a headline analyzer and a call-to-action optimization tool, which make it simple to write high-converting content.

Additionally, Copysmith provides a selection of templates for typical marketing pieces, including landing sites, ad Facebook advertising, a. One of the two giant systems for giant teams and businesses is Copysmith. They bought Rytr and Frase and have a Chrome extension and API access. This is the scalability platform. $19 per month for their base package (they also include a free trial)

4. Hypotenuse AI

The AI authoring tool Hypotenuse AI is gradually gaining popularity. Their content detective tool, which can be used to investigate and generate accurate material, their bulk content generator (ideal for product descriptions), and their AI picture generator are some of their standout features.

Like the other companies on this list, Hypotenuse AI creates creative material with a human-sounding voice using various language models. For editing, they also include a plagiarism and grammar checker.

Excellent all-purpose platform. The price for the base plan is $24 per month (they also have a free trial)

5. Copy AI is another AI text generator that uses GPT-3.

For those new to AI copywriting software, this one is simple to use, reasonably priced and has many ready-made templates. Additionally, it is continually updated with the most recent language models, resulting in consistently higher-quality output.

I enjoy using Copy AI to reuse my current material for social media postings. When creating original content for each platform and channel, it excels at leveraging templates to guide you in doing so (whether email newsletters, landing pages, or social media posts). Copy AI can write in more than 25 different languages. effective tool

Price: They provide a free plan for up to 2,000 words and one user seat on a subscription plan starting at $49/mon. For up to 40,000 words and five user seats.

Text to Image

Text to Image generators is based on Generative Adversarial Networks (GANs). These are designs where two neural networks compete against one another in a zero-sum scenario. Starting from random numbers, the Generator network elaborates realistic images, trying to deceive the Discriminator. First, the Discriminator network is trained to recognize pre-existing images through the analysis of millions of appropriately labeled examples, to understand whether those produced by the Generator are real or artificial. Then, gradually, from trial to trial, the Generator learns to make synthetic images that appear to have been created by a human.

The most advanced "text to image" systems, such as OpenAI and Imagen by Google, use "diffusion models." Both start from a model capable of understanding complex sentences, not simple keywords.

In the OpenAI system, these phrases are passed to calculators that use a model called "prior," which has the task of generating "CLIP image embedding" or "getting an idea" of those words (as happens to us humans when they ask us to draw a beach with umbrellas and boats on the horizon). Then these "CLIP image embedding" are passed to another network which, based on a "Decoder Diffusion model" (unCLIP), begins to draw that idea in successive steps.

Crayon

Crayon is a project born a few months ago by two developers who initially called it DALL-E Mini. Use a VQGAN template. It can be used for free, but only via the web, through a simple interface that allows you to enter the desired text. The output consists of nine downloadable but low-resolution images.

It works well with simple text, but the result will be messy if you try to create images involving multiple objects/subjects interacting.

Midjourney

- ◊ Midjourney is an independent research laboratory focused on design, human infrastructure, artificial intelligence, and the name of a very effective new Text-To-Image generator.
- ◊ The system is currently in beta and is accessible through a bot on Discord.
- ◊ The British Magazine the Economist used the software to create the cover for a June 2022 issue.
- ◊ The Midjourney team is led by David Holz, who previously co-founded Leap Motion and was a NASA research scientist.

Midjourney version 4

Midjourney version 4 introduced an awe-inspiring quality.

The Remix mode

Midjourney's Remix mode allows you to create image variations with intermediate prompts.

Imagen

Imagen is a Text-To-Image template from Google with unprecedented photorealism and a deep language understanding.

The key finding is that sizeable generic language models (e.g., T5), pre-trained on enormous amounts of textual content, are surprisingly effective at encoding text for image synthesis: increasing language model size in Imagen significantly increases both sample fidelity and image-text alignment.

In tests with real users, they preferred Imagen over other models regarding sample quality and image-text alignment.

Stable Diffusion

Another diffusion model created by Stability AI, CompVis LMU, and Runway is Stable Diffusion. The first public release is dated August 2022. Its code has been made available so it can be installed on your computer, a different approach from the other services. Those who don't want to take on this burden can use a browser interface called DreamStudio. When you first log in, you get credits to generate a set of images for free; then, you must pay for more.

Text to the video

The future is AI. Making films from any text is simple, thanks to AI video generators. Using an AI movie creator, you can quickly produce high-level films from the text that has a robotic presenter.

Stable Diffusion Videos

A free text-to-video AI generator online called Stable Diffusion Videos creates videos based on instructions. Below are some examples of videos:

Deforum Stable Diffusion

Text-to-video AI generator number two, Deforum, creates animations by building frames considering their ancestors. As a result, making cohesive films and animations using Stable Diffusion outputs with Deforum SD is easier than ever. For ideas, view the videos below:

Make-A-Video

Make-A-Video with just a few words, a new AI text-to-video generator from Meta, creates entertaining short videos.

The study is based on recent advancements in text-to-image producing technology and was conducted to allow text-to-video production. Movies may also be created using images and other types of videos and text. The diffusion is the same even though a time axis has been added.

The system learns how the world looks and how people usually talk about it using words and pictures. Unlabeled videos are another tool used to aid pupils in understanding how the world works.

You may utilize this knowledge to make amusing, creative videos that will help you bring your creativity to life with just a few words or lines of text.

VEED.io

You may easily create excellent web movies with VEED.io's powerful A.I. technology and user-friendly UI. Any text may be converted into movies or used as a video editor to cut, trim, add subtitles, and more.

This is how it works:

- ◊ Select a stock video or give one of your own.
- ◊ The video may be edited by adding text, images, etc.
- ◊ Save and export the film.

Lumen5

Lumen5 is an excellent web program for creating AI movies. More than 800,000 users use Lumen5 to create high-quality video content. Its ease of use and minimal requirement for video editing knowledge make it the finest. In addition, artificial intelligence allows you to swiftly develop films from scratch or scratch in a couple of minutes.

This is how it works:

- ◊ Enter some text or a script here.
- ◊ Lumen5 will automatically choose the best audio and visuals based on the screenplay.
- ◊ You can give your logos, music, and text.
- ◊ Download and share the film.

Designs.AI

Use the incredible AI-powered content production tool Design.AI to turn your blog posts and articles into captivating videos. In addition, you may quickly create logos, movies, and banners with its assistance.

This is how it works:

- ◊ First, insert your text or script.
- ◊ Select a sector.
- ◊ Pick a video style and voice that you like.
- ◊ After this, the AI will quickly create a video preview. After that, you may edit your video and enhance its aesthetic attractiveness by adding text and music.

Text to Audio

Artificial intelligence has made it possible to make excellent tools and generators that turn text into speech (AI). "Text to speech" is a voice synthesis program that looks at text and reads it aloud in a way that sounds like a person.

Text to Audio generators is employed in various contexts, such as voiceover by companies and artists, and an assistive tool for those with learning disabilities. These generators are also often used in audiobooks, branding, animation, and gaming, among other things. Also, because the industry changes quickly, the technology can work well with more audio samples or specialized tools.

Several excellent Texts to Audio software programs are available, each with a particular set of features and uses.

Synthesis

Synthesis is one of the most well-known influential time AI text-to-Audio generators; anybody can create a polished AI voiceover or movie with only a few clicks.

This platform is at the forefront of creating algorithms for videos with text-to-voiceover and usage in advertising. Imagine having a natural human voice available to improve your website, explainer films, or product tutorials in a few minutes. With the help of Synthesys Text-to-Video (TTV) and Text-to-Audio (TTA) technologies, your script may be turned into engaging media presentations. Numerous features are available, such as:

- Choose from many expert voices: 35 women and 30 men
- Anyone can make and sell as many voiceovers as they want for any reason.
  , Unlike rival platforms, the voices are incredibly lifelike.
- Use for letters, TV advertising, instructional videos, social media, podcasts, and more.

Murf

Murf, one of the market's most well-known and outstanding AI voice generators, is an excellent text-to-audio broaderator. Many professions, including product developers, podcasters, educators, and business executives, utilize Murf to enable anybody to convert text to Audio, voice-overs, and dictations.

Murf has several modification options to enable you to produce the most realistic-sounding voices. In addition, you may select from several agents and accents, and the UI is user-friendly.

The text to Audio generator gives customers access to a feature-rich AI voice-over studio with an integrated video editor, allowing you to produce voice-over videos. In addition, you may choose your preferences, such as Speaker, Accents/Voice Styles, Tone, or Purpose, from a pool of more than 100 AI voices that span 15 different languages.

The voice changer, which lets you record without using your voice as a voiceover, is another standout feature by Murf. Pitch, speed, and volume adjustments can all be made to Murf's voiceovers. In addition, you can alter pronunciation or add pauses and emphasis.

The following are some of Murf's best qualities:

- ◊ A sizable collection with more than 100 AI voices available in several languages
- ◊ Emotive expression in speech
- ◊ AI Voice-Over Studio supports both audio and text input.
- ◊ Tone, accents, and other aspects are all adjustable.

Lovo

Lovo, often used for gaming, audio advertisements, online learning, and audiobooks, is another of the best text-to-audio generators. People who want to use a voice different than their own are the target audience for the tool.

Lovo uses imported text converted to audio to produce natural voices using artificial intelligence (AI). Several of the best businesses in the world, like Nvidia, have used the text-to-voice generator.

With over 180 AI voice skins available in 33 languages, Lovo makes it simple to pick the ideal one. You can search by situations (games, advertisements, e-learning), character, gender, and accent (informative, trustworthy). You can type the script by hand or upload a pre-written file when making a voice-over.

The following are some of Lovo's key characteristics:

- ◊ Over 180 AI voice skins in 33 different languages

- ◊ individual voice skins
- ◊ Human feelings
- ◊ Cloning voices
- ◊ Write a script or upload one

Sonantic

Since the actor Val Kilmer employed a synthetic voice copy to help him restore his voice, Sonantic has gained more recognition. In addition, simple AI technology is well-liked in entertainment since it allows animated speech emotions.

You may use the tool to alter the tone of the created speech, choosing from options like cheerful, sad, or furious. It works by copying and pasting written text into the editor, then waiting for it to be converted to audio. You may even alter the amount of emotion. Sonantic has been employed in cartoons, movies, and video games for these reasons.

The following are some of Sonantic's best qualities:

- ◊ Voice generator that sounds human
- ◊ Emotional changes
- ◊ voice qualities
- ◊ voice initiatives like Fear or Shouts

Audio to Text

Several AI-based tools and techniques are available for converting audio to text, also known as speech recognition or automatic speech recognition (ASR). These services convert spoken utterances into written text using neural networks and machine learning techniques. Transcription quality depends on the quality of the audio input, the accent and the background noise of the speaker, and the training data used to develop the ASR model. Some of the most common ones include:

Google Speech-to-Text API: This cloud-based API converts spoken words into written text in more than 120 languages and variants. It can handle multiple speakers and recognize different accents and background noises.

Google gives users 60 minutes of free transcription, with $300 in free credits for Google Cloud hosting. However, since Google only supports transcribing files already in a Google Cloud Bucket, you will need more than the free credits to get you.

Amazon Transcribe: This cloud-based service can transcribe audio files in real time or from pre-recorded files. It supports multiple languages and can manage multiple speakers and different accents.

The automatic voice recognition service Amazon Transcribe turns audio files into text using machine learning algorithms. Adding speech-to-text functionality to any application or using Amazon Transcribe as a stand-alone transcription service are options.

You may enhance accuracy for your particular use case with language customization, filter material to protect customer privacy or audience-appropriate language, analyze information in multi-channel audio, divide the voice of different speakers, and more with Amazon Transcribe.

How Amazon Transcribe Works

Text from the speech is converted using Amazon Transcribe. A simple transcription request results in a transcript containing information about the transcribed content, such as confidence ratings and timestamps for each word and punctuation mark. Refer to the feature overview for a comprehensive list of features you may add to your transcription.

There are two primary groups of transcription techniques:

- ◊ Transcribing media files uploaded to an Amazon S3 bucket in batches.
- ◊ Real-time transcription of media streams is known as streaming transcription.

You may produce batch transcriptions using the AWS CLI, AWS Management Console, and AWS SDKs. In addition, you may produce streaming transcriptions using the AWS Management Console, HTTP/2, WebSockets, and other AWS SDKs.

Data Input and Output: Amazon Transcribe converts audio data into written data using a media file in an Amazon S3 bucket or a media stream. Conducting batch transcription tasks on media files stored in an Amazon S3 bucket differs from performing streaming transcriptions on media streams. Therefore, different guidelines and standards apply to these two procedures. Media formats Lossless formats are recommended for batch and streaming transcriptions, while the supported media types vary.

Sample Rates

The sample rate parameter is an optional one that you may use with batch transcribing projects. If you include it in your request, ensure the value you provide corresponds to the sample rate in your audio; otherwise, your job might fail. Your request for subscriptions must contain a sampling rate. Make sure the value you provide corresponds to the actual sample rate in your audio, just like with batch transcription jobs. For example, 8,000 Hz is the typical sample rate for low-fidelity audio, such as telephone recordings. Amazon Transcribe accepts values between 16,000 Hz and 48,000 Hz for high-fidelity audio.

Output

The output for transcription is in JSON format. The transcript is presented in paragraph form in the first section of your transcript, followed by additional information for each word and punctuation mark. The information you receive depends on the features you request. At the very least, your transcript must include each word's start time, end time, and confidence rating.

Amazon S3 buckets are used to store all batch transcripts. You can have Amazon Transcribe use a secure default bucket or save your transcript in your own Amazon S3 bucket. See Working with buckets for more information on creating and using Amazon S3 buckets.

When requesting transcription, including the URI of the Amazon S3 bucket where you want the transcript to be kept, ensure that Amazon Transcribe has to write rights for this bucket before beginning your batch transcribing project. Your transcript will stay in the designated bucket until you delete it.

Amazon Transcribe uses a secure service-managed bucket and gives you a temporary URI you may use to get your transcript if you don't specify an Amazon S3 bucket. The validity of temporary URIs is 15 minutes. Make a Get Transcription Job request to obtain a new temporary URI for your transcript if you see an Access Denied error when using the specified URI.

When your job expires, if you choose a default bucket, your transcript is removed (90 days). Therefore, you must download your f you wish to k it after this deadline.

Getting started with Amazon Transcribe

Before you can make transcriptions, you need to meet a few conditions:

◊ Create an AWS account

- ◊ Install the AWS CLI and SDKs (you can omit this step if you use the AWS Management Console for your transcriptions).
- ◊ Create IAM login credentials.
- ◊ Create a bucket in Amazon S3
- ◊ Establish an IAM policy.
- ◊ You are prepared to transcribe as soon as you have finished these requirements. To get started, choose your preferred transcription technique from the list below.
  - o AWS CLI.
  - o Management Console for AWS
  - o AWS SDK.
  - o HTTP
  - o WebSockets

IBM Speech-to-Text: This cloud-based service uses machine learning algorithms to transcribe audio into text. It can accommodate many speakers and accents and supports multiple languages.

IBM Speech to Text for IBM Cloud Pak for Data offers speech recognition capabilities for your applications. The service uses machine learning to accurately translate human speech by combining knowledge of grammar, linguistic structure, and the structure of audio and voice signals.

The IBM Watson® Voice to Text service offers speech transcription capabilities for your applications. The service uses machine learning to accurately translate human speech by combining knowledge of grammar, linguistic structure, and the structure of audio and voice signals. As more address is added, it continually updates and improves its transcription.

The service offers APIs that enable it to be used with any application that accepts voice as an input and outputs a text transcript. It may be applied to projects like multimedia transcription, analytical call center tools, and voice-activated chatbots. Among many other uses, voice control of embedded devices, transcribing meetings and conference calls, and dictating messages and notes are feasible.

Customers needing high-quality voice transcripts from call center audio should use this service. In addition, customers may create cloud-native apps for customer service, customer voice, agent support, and other solutions in sectors including financial services, healthcare, insurance, and communications.

Variations of Products

Speech to Text can be implemented locally or as a managed cloud service. Both product versions are covered in this documentation's instructions for usage. Topics, paragraphs, and examples that only apply to one edition of the document are explicitly marked:

IBM Cloud

For instances of Speech to Text managed and hosted on the IBM Cloud or the IBM Cloud Pak for Data as a Service.

IBM Cloud Pak for Data

Speech to Text for IBM Cloud Pak for Data instances deployed or hosted on-site. Visit Installing IBM Watson Speech to Text for IBM Cloud Pak for Data for connections to resources on installing and administering Speech to Text for IBM Cloud Pak for Data.

Speech Recognition

Three voice recognition interfaces are available through the Speech to Text service: an asynchronous HTTP interface, a WebSocket interface, and a synchronous HTTP interface. Using the interfaces, you may customize your audio's language, format, and sample rate. Additionally, they offer a wide range of settings that you may use to customize the audio requests you make and the information the service responds with. Further, you may ask for statistics on the audio's analysis by the service and the audio itself.

Customization

You may adjust voice recognition using the service's customization interface to suit your linguistic and acoustic needs. For example, you can add domain-specific terms to a model's vocabulary or modify it to account for your audio's acoustic properties.

Language assistance

> The service supports many dialects and languages:

- Arabic (Modern Standard) (Modern Standard)
- Chinese (Mandarin) (Mandarin)
- Czech
- Dutch (Belgian and Netherlands) (Belgian and Netherlands)
- English (Australian, Indian United Kingdom, United States) (Australian, Indian, United Kingdom, and United States)
- French (Canadian France) (Canadian, and France)
- German
- Hindi (Indian) (Indian)
- Italian
- Japanese
- Korean
- Portuguese (Brazilian) (Brazilian)
- Spanish (Castilian and Latin American) (Castilian and Latin American)
- Swedish

Audio Assistance

The service takes audio in a variety of well-known formats for transcription:

- ◊ Opus or Vorbis audio with Ogg or Web Media (WebM) audio MP3 (or MPEG)
- ◊ Format for Waveform Audio Files (WAV)
- ◊ Lossless audio codec for free (FLAC)
- ◊ 16-bit pulse-code modulation in linear form (PCM)
- ◊ A-Law Mu-Law G.729 (or u-law)

Microsoft Speech Services: This cloud-based platform includes speech recognition, text-to-speech, and translation services. It supports multiple languages and can manage various speakers and different accents.

Convert audio to text from various sources, such as microphones, audio files, and blob storage. Analyze the speaker's diary to find out who said what and when. Transcripts with automated formatting and punctuation are readable.

More than the standard model might be needed if there is much industry- and domain-specific jargon in the audio or the noise. You may use acoustic, linguistic, and pronunciation data to build and train specific speech models in these situations. Custom speech models can give you a competitive edge and are private.

Speech examples

Speech situations that are typical include:

- ◊ Learn how to apply profanity filters, get partial results, make modifications, sync captions with your input audio, and recognize spoken languages for multilingual settings.
- ◊ Audio Content Creation: Neural voices may improve in-car navigation systems, turn digital texts like e-books into

audiobooks, and make interactions with chatbots and voice assistants more natural and entertaining.
◊ Contact Center Redact personally identifiable information, transcribe conversations in real-time or as a batch, and extract insights like sentiment to support your call center use case.

Voice assistants: Develop conversational interfaces for their apps and experiences that are natural and human-like. The voice assistant function makes a fast, dependable, reliable device and an assistant implementation.

Kaldi ASR: This is an open-source toolkit for speech recognition that can be used to develop custom speech recognition systems. It is adaptable, scalable, and can be taught to understand different languages and accents.

An open-source toolkit for working with voice data is called Kaldi. However, it is also utilized for other tasks, such as speaker identification in voice-related applications. The toolkit existed for seven years, but a sizable community regularly updates and improves it. As a result, Kaldi is widely used in business and academia (400+ citations in 2015).

Although Bash and Python scripts cover the toolkit, Kaldi is primarily built in C/C++. This wrapper eliminates the need to delve too far into the source code for simple usage. I've learned about the toolkit and how to use it during the past five months. This article's objective is to walk you through that process and provide you with the resources that were most helpful to me. Consider it a shortcut.

Kaldi's Three Components

I. **Preprocessing and Feature Extraction**

Most audio data models use pixel-based data representation data. Use characteristics that are excellent for two things primarily when you wish to extract such a representation:

- ◊ Recognizing the human voice's sound
- ◊ Removing any extraneous sounds.
- ◊ Over the years, there have been several attempts to make these traits, but the industry now relies heavily on mocks.
- ◊ Mel-frequency cepstral coefficients, or mfcc, were developed by Mermelstein and Davis in the 1980s and have nearly become industry standards. Mfccs are better theoretically explained in this incredibly understandable paper. All you need to know for primary usage is that mocks only consider not audible to human ears.

Two more characteristics are used in Kaldi:

CMVNs are used to normalize better MFCC I-Vectors, which are utilized to comprehend the variations within the domain and require their page—making a speaker-dependent representation, for instance. JFA (Joint Factor Analysis) is built on the same principles. However, I-Vectors are more suited to comprehend channel and speaker variations.

II. The Model

BLAS and LAPACK (written in Fortran!) and an alternate GPU solution based on CUDA are used to construct the matrix algebra that powers Kaldi. Since Kaldi employs such low-level packages, it is incredibly effective at completing specific jobs.

The Kaldi model is made up of two primary parts:

- ◊ The Acoustic Model, once a GMM but now superseded mainly by Deep Neural Networks, is the first component. The model will convert the audio characteristics we constructed into a series of context-dependent phonemes, which we refer to as "pdf-ids" in Kaldi and represent numerically.

◊ The Decoding Graph, which takes phonemes and transforms them into lattices, is the second component. A lattice is a visual depiction of potential alternate word sequences for a given audio component. In most cases, this is the output you desire from a voice recognition system. The decoding graph considers the distribution and probability of contiguous individual words and the grammar of your data (n-grams).

The decoding graph is a WFST. Thus, I urge anyone looking to advance professionally to grasp this topic in depth. These movies and this historic essay are the simplest ways to accomplish it. After each concept, you can see how the decoding graph functions. The Kaldi project refers to this combination of many WFSTs as an "HCLG.fst file," it is built on the open-fast framework.

Worth Noting: The model's operation has been streamlined in this wConnecting the two models and expressing the phonemes using a decision tree is a somewhat involved process tree. Even so, this reduction can make it simpler for you to comprehend.

The Process of Training

Typically, the most challenging part is that your audio transcriptions must be ordered in Kaldi in an exact manner covered in detail in the guidelines.

Once you've ordered your data, you'll need a representation of each word to the phonemes that make it up. The outputs of the acoustic model will be determined by this representation, which we shall refer to as the "dictionary." Here is a sample of one of these dictionaries:

◊ eight -> ey t
◊ five -> f ay v

- ◊ four -> f an r
- ◊ nine -> n ay n

You may begin training your model after you have bose things in your possession—the various training techniques called Ledo as "recipes" in the Kaldi dialect. The run bash script might help you better grasp the WSJ recipe, which is the most often-used recipe.

In most recipes, we begin by using GMM to match the phonemes with the audio sound. This fundamental stage, dubbed "alignment," aids us in deciding what sequence we want our DNN to produce later.

We will build the will to make up the acoustic model after the alignment and train it to match the result. After constructing the acoustic model, we may train the WFST to convert the DNN output into the desired lattices.

How These Audio-To-Text AI Tools Work

Speech recognition algorithms use statistical models and machine learning techniques to transcribe audio into text. The models are trained on large datasets of speech and text and then used that training to transcribe new audio inputs. Some of the most popular algorithms used in speech recognition include Hidden Markov Models (HMMs), Gaussian Mixture Models (GMMs), and Deep Neural Networks (DNNs).

Natural Language Processing (NLP) techniques: These techniques are used to extract meaning from the transcribed text and to correct errors in the transcription. NLP techniques can recognize named entities, extract keywords and phrases, and perform sentiment analysis.

Acoustic models represent speech sounds and are used by speech recognition algorithms to transcribe audio into text. Acoustic models are trained on large datasets of speech and text and can be customized for different languages, accents, and speaking styles.

Language models: These models represent the structure and content of language and are used by speech recognition algorithms to transcribe audio into text. Language models are trained on large text datasets and can be customized for different languages and genres.

These audio-to-text AI systems have improved in accuracy and dependability recently to machine learning advancements and the accessibility of vast voice and text datasets result, they're widely utilized applications, such as voice-activated devices, closed captioning, and contact center transcription.

Field of Work Where Ai Could Be Beneficial

Marketing and Advertising

Data and AI are rapidly changing marketing and advertising, as it has in so many other businesses. Customers see these changes in the chatbots that help them make buying decisions as customized advertisements on their web browsers. But what do AI in marketing and advertising mean?

Artificial intelligence (AI) in advertising refers to emulating human intellect in devices designed to act and think as people based on the data proving them. They make better judgments in the future by using historical data to draw lessons from the past. Advertisers may utilize AI to make choices more quickly, target the right audience, and provide personalized experiences.

Artificial intelligence (AI) technologies are used in marketing to automate decisions generated from data collection, analysis, and further of audience or economic patterns that affect marketing efforts. In digital marketing campaigns where speed is crucial, AI is frequently deployed. AI marketing tools evaluate data and client profiles to determine the most effective interaction methods. They then send targeted communications at the right time without an assistant market item members team. Digital marketers of today use AI to assist marketing teams or complete more tactical tasks that don't require as much human skill.

Which Aspects of AI Are Used in Marketing and Advertising?

◊ **Capabilities of machine learning**

AI is the driving force behind cognitive advertising, which uses computer algorithms to evaluate information and automatically enhance the user experience. For example, machine-hire learning-enabled devices may consider new data using pertinent past data. Choices are then made depending on whether or not artificial intelligence, which is made up of computer algorithms that can evaluate data and automatically optimize digital marketing efforts based on experience, makes machine learning possible. Digital marketing activities can benefit from machine learning-enabled devices' examination of new data in the context of important historical data by educating them based on what has or hasn't worked in the past.

◊ **Using analytics and extensive data**

Big data has gained attention due to the rise of digital media. Additionally, it has allowed marketers to see how their efforts are valued across many channels. However, this has made it difficult for many marketers to choose which data sets are worthwhile to gather. Additionally, many marketers deal with data quality and information upkeep.

Due to the advent of "big data" brought on by the expansion of digital media, digital marketers can now grasp their efforts and accurately distribute value across channels. There is now a plethora of sult, and many digital marketers want assistance determining which data sets are valuable to purchase. AI marketing might help sort through all that data swiftly, distilling it to its most essential elements, assessing it, and recommending the most successful aspects for ensuing digital marketing initiatives.

◊ **Platforms for AI that work effectively**

A centralized platform for handling vast volumes of data may be made available to marketers through efficient AI technologies tools to make data-driven decisions more straightforwardly, which may generate valuable marketing analytics about your target audience.

Digital marketers have a unified platform for handling the enormous amounts of data collected thanks to efficient AI-powered marketing tools. In addition, these AI marketing solutions may provide helpful marketing insights about your target market, which you can use to successfully guide your data-driven decisions in contacting them. For instance, frameworks like Bayesian Learning and Forgetting can assist marketers in better assessing a customer's receptivity to a particular digital marketing endeavor.

How is Advertising Being Altered by AI?

Due to its wealth of advantages and capacity to become more intelligent over time, AI is quickly altering the advertising environment. Here are a few ways businesses may use AI in advertising.

◊ **Before serving advertisements, audiences might be segmenting machine learning and artificial intelligence; advertisers may discover trends based on audience behavior and message repronounces** to determine the sort of material a particular niche sector wants to view; machine learning considers all the data it has on a given person, including demographics and online activity. For example, the number one reason* why customers refrain from engaging more frequently is because of irrelevant material, which highlights the importance of understanding an audience.

According to a recent McKinsey Analytics survey, 14%* of users have implemented AI for customer segmentation objectives. More relevant advertising is produced due to proper segmentation and audience targeting. Advertisers should anticipate improved engagement rates and more conversions by providing relevant messaging to the end user.

◊ **The benefits of personalization improve consumer experiences.**

Advertising personalization uses data or consumer insights to make ads more relevant to their target audience. Data on demographics, interests, purchasing intentions, or behavioral patterns are some examples of this.

With 80%* of frequent customers indicating they only do business with businesses that tailor their experience, making advertisements more relevant and personalized is quickly becoming a primary focus. 56% of customers want their interactions with brands or suppliers to be individualized, and 47%* of B2C consumers say businesses could better match their engagement activities with their preferences.

Advertisers may enhance their relationships with customers, strengthen their bond with their brand, and improve the purchasing experience by using a customized AI solution like conversational marketing. Since 71%* of customers want companies to interact with them in real-time, using an AI conversational marketing solution to connect with customers and prospects has become more common. As a result, brands benefit from personalized experiences by increasing ROI and fostering stronger customer bonds.

◊ **AI-generated ads convert more effectively.**

AI can provide insights that guide advertising decisions and make sure that cash isn't wasted on ad text that doesn't convert by being able to look at historical trends and performances. AI does this by going beyond conventional A/B testing and using data to forecast how well-received content and message will be by customers. This enables advertisers to adopt a proactive strategy instead of a reactive one to produce more quality leads and conversions.

According to a recent Salesforce Research titled "Enterprise Technology Trends,"* 83% of IT leaders believe that AI and machine learning are changing how customers connect with brands, and 69% believe it is changing how they do business. As a result, advertisers and the importance of targeting the correct audience with the proper message increase conversions.

◊ **AI Can produce a More Interactive Experience.**

Real-time client interactions may be used to customize campaigns using interactive marketing techniques like conversational marketing. Chatbots replicate the in-person experience on your digital platforms and ecosystem using conversational AI and machine learning. These interactions are tailored to your customer's desires and needs, improving their online experience.

◊ **Targeting and budget optimization are also affected by performance optimization.**

The effective use of AI in advertising is performance optimization. Machine learning algorithms evaluate how well your advertisements work across various platforms and provide suggestions for better performance.

How to Market with AI

When implementing AI in marketing campaigns and business processes, starting with a well-thought-out approach is critical. This will guarantee that marketing teams avoid expensive problems and maximize their AI investment in the shortest period. There are a few critical issues for digital marketers to think about before deploying any AI marketing tools:

◊ **Decide on goals**

Your AI marketing campaign should start with well-defined goals and marketing data, just like any other marketing initiative. Then, start by finding areas inside campaigns or processes that, for example, segmentation, should be enhanced. Thus, it is essential to establish precise KPIs, particularly for qualitative goals like "improving customer experience," which can help to demonstrate the success of an AI-augmented marketing campaign.

◊ **Data Privacy Guidelines**

When you launch your innovative marketing campaign with the goal of data personalization, be sure your AI marketing platform will adhere to accepted guidelines for data usage. To ensure compliance and customer confidence, ensure privacy guidelines are defined and programmed into your AI marketing platforms as necessary.

◊ **Quantity and Sources of Data**

Digital marketers often need access to a large quantity of data before using AI marketing. Using this information, the marketing AI tool will be educated about customer preferences, external trends, and other factors influencing AI-enabled marketing campaigns' performance. The company's own CRM, information from previous marketing campaigns, and website data may all be used to gather this information. Marketers Marketing this with second and third-party data, such as location information, weather information, and other unrelated components influencing a consumer's purchasing choice.

◊ **Develop Your Data Science Talent**

When marketing businesses need to hire more personnel with the necessary data science and AI knowledge, dealing with massive amounts of data and providing insights could be challenging. To train their tools for the most outstanding performance and to make ongoing maintenance easier, organizations should collaborate with external parties who can assist with data collecting and analysis to launch AI marketing campaigns.

◊ **Maintain data quality**

As they analyze more data, machine learning and AI marketing systems will become more capable of making decisions. However, your AI marketing program's insights will only be beneficial if the data it uses is correct and standardized; otherwise, it can even influence decisions that hurt rather than enhance your bottom line. Therefore, before implementing AI marketing initiatives, marketing teams must work with data management and other business lines to develop data cleaning and upkeep procedures. When doing so, keep in mind the following seven crucial data dimensions:

- Promptness
- Completion
- Resilience
- Pertinence
- Openness.
- Precision

◊ **Develop a comprehensive AI marketing strategy.**

Most digital marketers believe their AI marketing solutions are highly beneficial when employed with an existing marketing plan rather than as a highly only method. It is possible to automate labor-intensive or error-prone procedures, including data analysis or attribution, using AI marketing tools.

Digital marketers may build on the foundation of effective digital marketing methods they have already used by incorporating AI to fill in these "blind spots" and elevate their marketing via these powerful, forward-thinking strategies.

Advantages of AI in Advertising

Although it is still a relatively new field of research, artificial intelligence offers a vast array of potential applications. Additionally, the advertising sector finds the usage of AI in advertising beneficial. The following are some

Advantages of AI in Advertising:

1. Use Data to More Effectively Target Your Ads
   Advertisers are continuously searching for fresh and efficient approaches to target their adverts. As a result, extensive data usage has been received recently to enhance ad targeting. Big data is an enormous amount that can now be accessed thanks to digital technology. Using this information, tailored advertisements may be made based on predicted customer preferences and behavior. According to Forbes, the most current study suggests that a mix of AI and big data can automate up to 80% of all physical work, 70% of data processing acdata-collecting4% of data collecting chores.

2. Helps in campaign optimization for improved outcomes
   Digital marketing is using artificial intelligence more and more since it can help campaigns be optimized for better outcomes. AI can determine what aspects of a campaign are effective and ineffective and alter them accordingly. Optimized and created campaigns with the audience's requirements to increase consumer engagement and retention. Additionally, it gives businesses a higher ROI.

3. Contributes to Time and Money Savings and Increased Sales
   Due to its ability to quickly classify the vast volumes of data that are now accessible, AI can help you save time and money. Additionally, it finds trends and patterns that help with better advertising choices. AI is being used by businesses like Amazon

to drive pricing tactics that help to lower prices for more sales. They have also used AI to comprehend and take advantage of pricing methods, such as raising the price of a product in response to rising demand. As a result, it helps businesses in increasing sales and income.

4. Lower Your Chances of Advertising Losses

    You may lessen the amount of money you would typically lose if your marketing campaign had an error by employing AI to help you determine which advertisements are most likely to result in a sale is one advantage of using AI for marketing initiatives. This enables companies to concentrate on advertising with the best chance of success, saving time and money that might be squandered on unsuccessful campaigns. AI also has the advantage of helping in the early detection of prospective dangers throughout a campaign. As a result, businesses may reduce risks by identifying dangers early.

5. Increasing Customer Satisfaction

    Better client communication and more individualized service are both possible with AI. It may assist businesses in getting to know their clients, understanding their wants and preferences, and then forecasting their future behavior. It enables companies to provide clients with excellent, individualized services and goods. As an illustration, consider the time Nike used AI to let customers customize their sneakers in-store. They gathered more information and used it to inform the design of future items. For clients more inclined to purchase when they believe their preferences are being effectively taken care of, such AI-backed advertising approaches are essential.

6. Expand Your Customer Base Through Your Ads

    Finding new, creative methods to connect with your target audience is more important than ever in social media. AI may help you better target your adverts by identifying what works and doesn't. For example, the largest beverage corporation,

Coca-Cola, examined 120,000 social media information to understand demographics and consumer behavior. They also looked at clients who actively discussed their brand and goods. Therefore, by comprehending data from prior initiatives, AI may assist businesses in honing the messages they wish to convey to the public. It can also identify patterns and trends through beneficial practical roving advertising selections.

7. Setting the Customer Journey

   The way organizations engage with their consumers evolves along with technology. AI is beneficial for defining and tracking a customer's journey via an advertisement. The following advertising may then benefit from this knowledge. It is possible to achieve this by keeping track of the websites that clients have visited, the items they have looked up, or the advertisements they have clicked on. AI may also monitor how users respond to advertising. It includes tracking their viewing duration, the areas of the ad they are paying attention to, and whether they are clicking on any links.

Advantages of Using Artificial Intelligence (AI) in Marketing

Different use cases for incorporating AI marketing may benefit your digital marketing initiatives, and each use case offers benefits. AI marketing may help businesses in several ways, including lowering risk, speeding up processes, increasing customer happiness, and generating more income. Benefits may be quantified (based on sales volume) or not (user satisfaction). There are a few universal benefits that apply to all uses of AI in marketing:

1. An increased campaign ROI

   When appropriately applied, AI marketing may alter a marketer's marketing strategy by sifting through their datasets to find the essential information and acting on it in real-time. For example, AI technologies can quickly decide how to split spending across media channels or look at the best ad locations to make campaigns more effective and keep customers interested.

2. Real-time personalization and improved customer relationships
AI marketing could help you send customized messages to clients at the right time in their customer lifecycle. Also, it could help digital marketers find clients who are at risk so they can send them messages to get them interested in the company again.

3. Enhancements in Marketing Measurement
It might take some time to pinpoint the performance of specific initiatives since many firms need help to keep up with the amount of data that digital marketing initiatives produce. However, through AI market ting dashboards, it is possible to grasp what is realistic in greater detail, reproduce it across channels, and allocate resources effectively.

4. Speed up decision-making
AI marketing uses machine learning and tactical data analysis to make decisions faster than humans can, depending on the campaign and the customer. Team members now have more time to concentrate on strategic initiatives that will use AI to assist in steering campaigns in the future. With AI marketing, digital marketers can choose the best media before the end of a campaign. Instead, they may make judgments based on real-time data.

Finance and Accounting

Artificial intelligence (AI) is now essential in many of the world's most competitive businesses. For example, the accounting and financial sectors have had a spectacular influence Ainfluencech is also revolutionizing how they work, creating new goods and services. As a result, the face of accounting and finance is fast altering due to recent advances in AI.

Audits, banking, tax preparation, bookkeeping, reporting, and payroll are just a few of the labor-intensive and time-consuming financial and accounting operations that have been efficiently automated with AI. Emerging technologies will be used to create self-learning systems incorporated into accounting duties. These systems will do repetitive and time-consuming operations, leaving people to handle managerial and analytical responsibilities. AI significantly influences everything from chatbots to actively managing the management accountant, from dealing with customer rules and needs to performing time-consuming duties.

According to Forbes, several reputable software providers, including Intuit, Sage, OneUp, and Xero, provide automated data input and reconciliation alternatives for organization bookkeeping using Machine Learning (ML) and Artificial Intelligence (AI) technology. Consequently, Chartered Professional Accountant experts have hired a new type to effectively and efficiently manage all the activities.

AI's Role in Accounting and Finance

Industry 4.0 is being shaped by innovative technologies in every sector with deft answers to the shifting demands of clients, suppliers, vendors, and partners. With automation, workers may do various repetitive jobs in between 80 and 90% less time than they used to. Lowering human mistakes also improves the output's quality.

AI has automated almost all accounting processes, including payroll, tax, banking, and audits, upending the accounting sector and bringing about a significant shift in how the company is conducted.

While increasing transparency and audibility, AI also increases output quality and productivity. In addition, AI opens a wide range of possibilities and reduces the traditionally time-consuming tasks of the finance team, allowing them to consider additional potential locations for business growth.

Accurate financial statement forecasting is made more accessible by AI. Finance experts may use machine learning (ML) and past data/records to forecast future trends.

RPA, which automates repeated work in corporate processes, is incredibly effective at doing repetitive tasks like document or data processing. The finance staff can only get slowed down by non-value-added duties now that RPA is in place. They should instead concentrate more on assuming strategic and advising roles.

RPA and Intelligent Automation applications in accounting:

- ◊ AI generates real-time analysis by analyzing documents using computer vision and natural language processing. As a result, the company can be proactive and modify the courses as needed by providing information through such reports to improve internal accounting operations like purchasing, invoicing, purchase orders, expense reports, accounts payable and receivables, etc.; AI enables the processing and automatic authorization of documents.
- ◊ By monitoring the relevant documents and issuing necessary alarms, enabled solutions to facilitate audits and compliance with business, state, and federal requirements.

- ◊ To prevent revenue loss, ML algorithms sift through vast amounts of data, detect possible fraud concerns, and flag them for review.

How to Use AI in Finance and Accounting?

Businesses that jump on the digital transformation bandwagon have an edge since they can use AI to enhance all facets of accounting, including operational effectiveness, cost savings, and ROI. For illustration:

- ◊ Processing of Payables and Receivables
  Invoice processing is one of the business processes that takes the most time and effort. AI-based invoice management solutions are beneficial because they boost volume, provide error-free processing, and enhance vendor relations.

- ◊ Onboarding of Suppliers
  With little to no human involvement, the AI-based strategy lets clients contact more people, generate more money, and assess suppliers.

- ◊ Processes for Purchasing
  The documentation is associated with purchasing and procurement procedures, sometimes spread across several systems outside the domain. Finance teams can manage unstructured data while automatically reducing governance, compliance, and risks using AI-driven processes.

- ◊ Auditability
  As RPA and analytics make it easier to follow regular transactions, data analytics sets the audit's scope and risk assessment. Tracking increasingly complicated transactions that include estimates and judgments is made possible by cognitive computing, predictive analytics, and AI.

- ◊ Monthly and quarterly cash flows

Thanks to AI-based solutions, businesses can quickly reconcile financial transactions, understand historical cash flows, and predict future cash requirements. AI apps collect data from several sources and integrate the data to guarantee the security of all financial activities.

- ◊ Financial Management
  Managing operations linked to costs manually involves much-complicated paperwork and is also vulnerable to fraud and data breaches. Expense management automation assures virtually no mistakes and notifies the team of a breach should it happen.

- ◊ Chatbot Assistance
  Chatbots powered by AI can swiftly and effectively answer user questions about account balances, financial statements, account status, and other topics. Accounts are kept in balance and closed on time by tracking unpaid bills and automating the subsequent collection operations. Additionally, AI chatbots may offer level 1 help and respond to common inquiries from clients.

Healthcare

Artificial intelligence (AI) is being applied increasingly in different areas, and the area focused on health is no exception. In this area, applications combine processing power with the knowledge and experience of experts in the medical field to facilitate tasks such as diagnosis, hospital administration, care, and surgeries, among other applications.

The COVID-19 pandemic taught us that we must bring together areas of expertise and specialized personnel from around the world to speed up vaccine development times. The other application areas also need the synergy of medical experts, data science, biotechnologists, and artificial intelligence to improve the processes involved in patient care, diagnosis, treatment, and monitoring.

AI is now a priority for healthcare decision-makers, governments, entrepreneurs, innovators, and specialists. Governments in a rising number of nations, including Finland, Germany, the United Kingdom, Israel, China, and the United States, have established goals for AI in healthcare. Many are making significant investments in research using AI. With VC financing for the top 50 businesses in healthcare-related AI exceeding USD 8.5 billion USD and giant tech corporations, startups, pharmaceutical and medical device companies, and health insurers dedicated to the AI healthcare ecosystem, the private sector continues to play an essential role.

The ways AI is changing the healthcare industry are:

◊ Research in new medicines:
The California Biomedical Research Association says that it takes a drug an average of 12 years to get from a research lab to a patient. Only one of the five medications that make it to human testing out of the 5,000 that go through preclinical testing is authorized for use in people. The average cost for a business to deliver a new medicine from the research lab to the patient is USD 359 million.

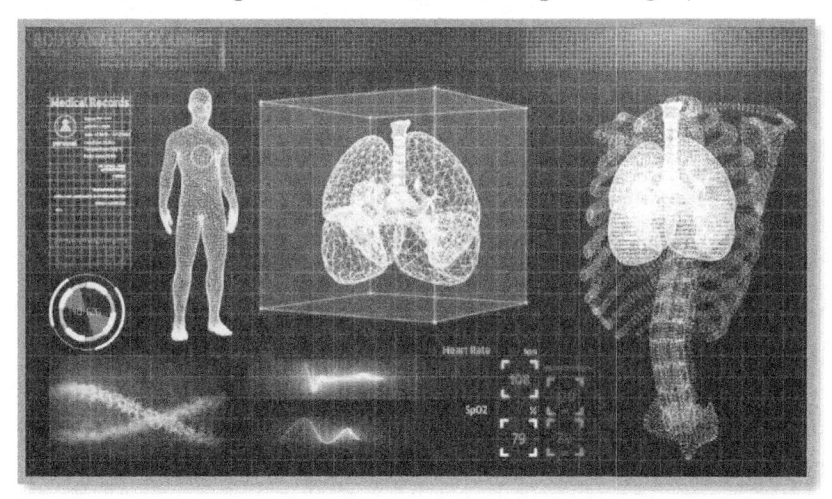

One of the most recent uses of AI in the healthcare industry is drug discovery. As a result, there is the potential to drastically shorten the time to market for new panels and their prices by utilizing the most recent developments in AI to expedite the drug discovery and drug repurposing processes.

One example is Pfizer, using IBM Watson, which uses machine learning, to search for the next generation of treatments.

◊ Diagnosis:

Through the analysis of large volumes of structured and unstructured data, it is possible to review the information to make accurate prognoses and diagnoses based on the history and behavior of the patient.

One example is Google's DeepMind Health, which works with doctors, researchers, and patients to solve real-world health problems.

◊ Decision making:

Improving care requires putting together a lot with the right decisions at the right time. Predictive analytics can help with clinical findings and actions and put administrative tasks in order of importance.

AI is also starting to get a foothold in medicine by using pattern recognition to find patients at risk of getting a disease or to see how it worsens due to lifestyle, environment, genetics, or other factors—medical attention.

◊ Virtual assistants:

AI-powered chatbots and machine learning-powered virtual assistants assist patients with conditions that make it challenging to access healthcare. These citizens can connect to virtual health assistants known as intelligent virtual assistants (IVAs) or virtual medical assistants (MVAs) to receive almost the same level of care as they would if they were sitting in a doctor's office.

As more people find a need for them, virtual assistants are being employed increasingly often in the United States.

◊ Treatment:
AI can assist doctors in managing patients' diseases more holistically, coordinating care plans, and helping patients in managing and adhere to their treatment regimens.

In addition, robots are also being adopted in surgeries that can help surgeons perform operations with high accuracy. The applications are diverse but focused on providing better care and increasing patients' quality of life.

Manufacturing and Logistics

AI (Artificial Intelligence) impacts many industries and fields, but advancements are poised to move logistics and manufacturing significantly. As a result, the field's technology has enormous potential utility.

In the late 1970s, AI was implemented in the manufacturing sector. But until 1997, only a little changed. Garry Kasparov was defeated in 1997 by Deep Blue, an AI-powered computer. After that, manufacturers understood that machines—not people—were the key to production, efficiency, and profitability. Since then, manufacturing AI has advanced at a startlingly rapid rate.

What does artificial intelligence in manufacturing mean?

Artificial intelligence (AI) describes the techniques that allow computers to do "intelligent" tasks with superhuman speed and accuracy—without requiring human input. Machine learning (ML), a field closely connected to artificial intelligence, is the study of convincing computers to do tasks without being explicitly taught.

The topic of artificial intelligence in logistics is expanding quickly and has the potential to change how businesses run significantly. Leading companies in the sector are creating cutting-edge solutions for driverless cars and other novel technology. These advancements bring several benefits, including increased efficiency in management duties like order fulfillment, greater inventory accuracy, quicker delivery times, and more accurate forecasting models.

What Function Does AI Have in the Manufacturing Industry?

Here are some ways in which artificial intelligence can be used in manufacturing:

- ◊ The first step would be to show the AI how people complete a task to educate it on how to do it. If done this way, the expansion will continue while also making progress. It can learn independently and accomplish various activities without continual supervision with enough time and practice.
- ◊ Crowdsourcing is the inevitable progression. This approach lets you get information from the broader public to train an AI. It can quickly complete this and compare the outcomes to previously recorded data. The end outcome will be an AI that can "hive mind," or know what everyone else knows, and has access to collective knowledge.
- ◊ Unsupervised learning makes it possible to supervise AI for the first time. This implies that it can learn things without being explicitly told to. How exactly will it recognize new information? They would apply a process known as reinforcement learning.

The Role of Artificial Intelligence in Logistics

- Authentic Vehicles

Although autonomous cars have received much attention, logisticians can automate other goods-transporting vehicles, like vans, lorries, and buses. In addition, self-driving cars can work independently or with a human driver.

This car can't drive itself yet, however. Automobile vehicles that don't have a human behind the wheel are not allowed on public roads right now. Legislation and technological constraints are to blame for this. Many countries still have laws that say the driver must be in the driver's seat to control traffic and look for possible dangers, but this will likely change.

This sort of technology can significantly improve logistics. Automated vehicles change the supply chain and save time and money. But what's more important is that autonomous technology might help reduce accidents. It also helps the environment because it uses less gasoline.

- Automation in the Warehouse Using Artificial Intelligence

This year, there are both new problems and possible solutions. Many multinational companies put money and time into robotics and AI technology because they need logistics solutions that are fast and smart. A lot of tedious tasks are made more accessible in warehouses by using automation. AI is revolutionizing warehousing operations, including data collection, analysis, and inventory management, allowing businesses to operate more effectively and generate more income.

AI is used in warehouses to predict demand, change orders, and reroute goods that are already on their way. With these predictions, you can change your orders and ensure that popular items are sent to warehouses nearby. In addition, if there is more than one warehouse in the chain, AI can connect them to determine the best way to move the inventory. As a result, you may enhance your service, save shipping expenses, and make significant financial savings when you estimate the demand for products and organize the logistics well in advance. The identification and arrangement of things are made possible using computer vision technologies in warehousing. This kind of technology will aid with quality control in the future and do away with human supervision requirements.

- Advanced Roads
Smart highways are another way that logistics companies use artificial intelligence. Several businesses are building them. Smart roads make driving safer, reduce delays in the supply chain caused by bad weather, and speed up deliveries.
Intelligent roads have things like solar panels and LED lighting. Solar panels are used to make electricity and keep roads from getting slippery in the winter because they can heat up. LED lights let drivers know when there are changes on the road. Businesses that use smart roads to move their goods can learn much from the information these roads provide. Fiber-optic sensor-equipped routes connected to the internet may be able to figure out traffic patterns and volumes and warn cars that a traffic jam is coming. They can tell when a vehicle is about to leave the road or when an accident is about to happen and let the right people know.

◊ A Better Prediction of Demand
Running a successful business depends on foreseeing future requirements for the number of products and supplies. When their estimates are erroneous, and the quantity of goods produced needs to be increased to meet the high demand, businesses lose money, which is the last thing they want to do. If your projections are on track, you run tracking out of inventory and lose sales. If you can't meet their needs, your customers will feel free to visit your competitors.

Algorithms made using artificial intelligence are available to forecast these tendencies. Some AI-based systems can predict what will happen even better than human experts, which leads to smaller inventories and easier management of warehouses. AI in logistics is also good because it makes the customer experience better. AI can ensure customers have a better experience by personalizing their experience and suggesting products based on their buying habits and interests. Customers that receive better-tailored expertise from a company will be more loyal to that company.

◊ Back Office Activities

Operations in the back office are essential to the logistics sector. AI significantly impacts how quickly and accurately numerous back-office tasks may be completed.

Cognitive automation is a technique that was developed by fusing AI with robotic process automation (RPA). When used with RPA, AI enables workers to perform better by boosting productivity and accuracy. For example, AI may be used to automate tedious data-related tasks. Back-office automation facilitates time and money savings for supply chain organizations. This technology can eliminate job categories, including accountants and human resource specialists. There will be fewer opportunities for human mistakes as a result.

What are AI's Manufacturing Benefits?

1. An increase in engineers' productivity

Streamlining calculations and most complex a load of even the most complicated mathematical issues. It automates these tasks or compiles them into user-friendly, occasionally no-code tools that engineers with different experience levels can utilize to speed up their work processes.

AI applications boost employee productivity by delivering crucial insights and automating tedious tasks. As a result, employees may focus more on the more creative aspects of their jobs and spend less time on routine tasks thanks to AI automation, which boosts job satisfaction and allows them to reach their full potential.

2. An inventive and influential design process (generative design)

AI drives software that can independently produce production-level designs. It alters the landscape. It does so based on the objectives and characteristics (spatial, materials, costs, etc.) entered by a designer or engineer and a corporation's existing and historical product catalog. The program generates several combinations for the operator to choose from using a technique called generative design, and it learns from each iteration to enhance future performance.

3. A better experience for the consumer

It can be challenging to differentiate on price or product in many industries because numerous manufacturers produce essentially the same items (margins are already razor-thin with escalating costs and global competition.) So the obvious next step is to differentiate yourself by providing clients with a superior experience.

4. More accurate forecasting of demand and inventory levels

Most manufacturers have felt the pain of having too much or too little inventory at critical times, which results in lost sales and indirectly drives customers toward rivals. Since inventory management has so many variables, humans often need help to get it right. Though AI can.

The nearly infinite computational capacity of AI makes maintaining adequate stock levels feasible. As a result, astonishingly complicated worldwide supply chains may be managed by manufacturers using AI to estimate demand, dynamically change stock levels between various sites, and control inventory movement.

According to McKinsey Digital, forecasting with AI can cut supply chain network failures by as much as 50%. In addition, it cuts warehouse expenditures by 10 to 40% and decreases missed revenues from out-of-stock by 65%. The projected costs of AI's effects on the supply chain are between $1.2T to $2T in manufacturing and supply chain planning. That is important.

5. Better quality assurance

The quality control procedure may be more affordable and swifter than in the past, thanks to AI's superior accuracy, imperviousness, and speed compared to humans. By detecting defects that humans would miss on a microscopic scale, AI can increase productivity and defect detection by 90%.

A lot of the time, using AI in manufacturing eliminates the requirement for quality control. Because AI is not fallible like humans, it can either fix mistakes as they happen or, for more excellent product quality, produce products that are practically guaranteed error-free.

6. Predictive upkeep
Predictive maintenance tracks the health of the machinery in manufacturing plants and forecasts when a repair is necessary (hint: before faults occur). The downtime and unnecessary routine maintenance costs are decreased using predictive analytics.
Predictive maintenance is more effective thanks to AI and machine learning. To achieve significant cost reductions, the technology combines massive amounts of data from sensors in machinery (detection of heat, vibration, movement, noise, etc.), computer vision, and even external data like the weather and the health of other connected machines.

According to data from the U.S. Department of Energy, predictive maintenance can save 8% to 12% over preventive care and save downtime by 35% to 45%. In addition to having a favorable financial impact, extending the life of machinery and reducing unplanned shutdowns benefits the environment.

AI's Advantages in Logistics

AI technology continues to disrupt the logistics industry profoundly to speed up shipments. Artificial intelligence's role in logistics has many benefits (AI). Every step of the logistics process can be aided by artificial intelligence.

1. Reliable Inventory Control

Artificial intelligence-driven technologies have much potential for inventory management due to their ability to manage massive amounts of data. The order in which products enter and leave a warehouse can be helped by accurate inventory management. Many inventory-related factors include order processing, picking, and packing, which can take a long time and be error-prone. Effective inventory control can help prevent overstocking, understocking, and unexpected stockouts.

2. Boost Storage Facility Efficiency

Artificial intelligence is changing warehouse processes, including data collecting and analysis, inventory management, and allowing firms to operate more effectively and earn more money. In warehousing, AI estimates demand, modifies orders, and reroutes goods in transit. You may change your order placements in response to these projections and arrange to deliver in-demand items to nearby warehouses. In addition, AI can connect the chain's many warehouses to find the most effective way to move the inventory if there are several. When demand for a particular product is predicted, and logistics are properly thought out, you can offer better customer service and spend less on warehousing.

3. Delivery on Time

AI systems can speed up, secure, and improve processes by reducing the need for manual labor. This makes it possible for the customer to fulfill their order and adhere to the terms of the contract. Artificial intelligence is used in logistics to enable on-time delivery through intelligent roads. Intelligent roads' improved contribution to road safety and their avoidance of logistical issues and delays brought on by adverse weather result in faster delivery. Sensor-equipped roads can monitor traffic numbers and patterns and warn cars of imminent gridlock.

Customer Service

Artificial intelligence (AI) radically alters how we operate in many industries. Whether in retail, banking, industry, or law, customer service has long been a part of these sectors. But, according to experts, it may become impossible to distinguish between a human and an AI bot in the upcoming years.

As companies attempt to streamline operations, AI-based contact center management systems like CommBox are becoming the norm. It makes it feasible for technology to help people in a way that is both economical and encourages the best client experience. The customer service revolution has only been accelerated by the more significant investments made in the sector by major digital giants like Google, Microsoft, and Facebook.

Early implementations of AI in customer service have demonstrated its capacity to lower costs, enhance staff loyalty and retention, boost revenue, and foster customer pleasure. Given all those incredible advantages, complete industry-wide adoption of the technology appears all but inevitable.

Ways AI can improve customer service

1. Customer service using chatbots

Today's customer service personnel must respond to numerous consumer calls daily. They must also work to cut down on the typical resolution time for each customer. Chatbots can help in part with both issues. Chatbots can respond to consumer inquiries in real-time and with lightning-quick accuracy. By responding to many client inquiries, they may also reduce the workload of human customer support employees. By 2020, more than 85% of client interactions will be managed automatically, predicts Gartner.

2. Cost-cutting and resource management

According to IBM, companies worldwide spend over $1.3 trillion annually on 265 billion customer support calls. Chatbots can help firms save customer care expenses by quickening response times, freeing up staff for more complex tasks, and answering up to 80% of simple queries. Call computerization is a prime example of this. It combines machine learning and enhanced speech recognition to enhance traditional interactive voice response systems while achieving cost savings of 60% to 80% compared to outsourced call centers run by humans.

3. Constant, year-round assistance

Customers prefer flexible service. All year, brands must be accessible to consumers and responsive to their needs. It may be made possible through automated customer support. It enables businesses to provide always-on customer care and handle problems as they come up. Customers may now get answers to their questions whenever they need them, day or night. This would not only significantly improve customer satisfaction and customer service, but it would also enhance brand reputation and foster more customer loyalty.

4. Better consumer connections with people

A significant part in enhancing human interactions with clients can be played by artificial intelligence. AI-augmented messaging and email tagging are the most central ways AI improves customer service. Thanks to AI-augmented messaging, customer care representatives can handle many customer inquiries with chatbot assistants. Additionally, AI email tagging enables people to save time by reducing the need to read every customer's email by having AI-powered algorithms scan emails, tag them, and direct them to the relevant office. As a result, customer care representatives can focus on the more challenging jobs that require human interaction while also saving time.

5. Individualized user experiences

According to research, 71% of customers prefer to address customer service issues independently. AI has great promise to help clients discover the correct information more quickly. With the help of artificial intelligence, it is possible to analyze consumer data and essential metrics and offer products or services to customers depending on their preferences for browsing and making purchases. AI can evaluate large data sets, which may also be utilized to detect location and weather information and provide clients with pertinent content. By creating client personas, businesses may concentrate on the specific purchasing behaviors of each customer and improve their understanding of them. They may give clients pertinent material via the proper channels at the correct times. Customers can thereby resolve issues without contacting customer care.

6. Collection of data

AI simplifies and unifies data collecting to produce a single customer view based on the consumers' behavioral patterns. Artificial intelligence initially depended on client data already gathered and manually provided. Modern AI-powered platforms are better at proactively requesting data from client data engagement. They can recognize trends in client behavior quickly and readily and respond to their needs and emotions. They are prompt in their responses and know when to probe further. AI systems may gather the relevant data, evaluate it, and take further steps to help customers as they make purchases. Businesses that have included AI in their systems are now benefiting from data collection and storage, which also helps to cut down on real-time procedures with no human participation.

7. Prognostications

Businesses must develop experiences that stick with their clients and become a part of their life. Predictive personalization customers believe every company, service, and product is made with them in mind. Providing clients with irrelevant information illnesses that have integrated AI into their systems has improved client relationships. Transparency and communication have improved as a result. AI's predictive insights have helped their work by making it easier to quickly look through previous items, inventory, or services to propose goods relevant to the consumer. Customer interactions and experiences will be streamlined across all channels using AI that includes e, including sights from client data that are nuanced

With the introduction of AI in customer analytics, organizations may uncover complex customer information. Data mining used to be laborious and time-consuming before the advent of AI. AI-powered systems can now process enormous volumes of data, evaluate it, and acquire insights, presenting new opportunities for organizations. For example, brands may utilize AI to evaluate every customer action, identify their interests, and use this information to create efficient, customized marketing campaigns. They can anticipate problems and determine the wants and needs of clients. For instance, goods and services can be placed in shops where people are most inclined to hang around. AI may assist businesses in driving results, providing important insights, eliminating human bias and error, and freeing up human resources for other work.

8. Supporting consumer decision-making

Approximately 80% of clients think AI-powered chatbots help them make better purchasing decisions than people. Customers now interact with brands across devices. Therefore, individualized touchpoints are necessary to support the customer's decision-making process. Automated AI-powered assistants quickly reply to consumer inquiries, gather in-depth details about the goods or services, and offer recommendations to help customers choose wisely. Humans spend less time doing this, freeing them up to complete other jobs finding and presenting answers, and expediting the settlement process. When interactions between the consumer and chatbot become complicated, a human agent takes over. Thanks to their machine-learning capabilities, bots can deliver precise solutions to a specific problem by learning from recurrent issues. Additionally, it can recognize trends in human behavior, which is advantageous for customers and agents.

Task management was made more accessible.

Bots with artificial intelligence (AI) or other systems used in customer care can manage many jobs at once. As a result, the way that brands and customers connect has evolved. For example, due to having to wait so long for a customer executive to address their problem, 52% of consumers hung up on the customer support line, and about 50% of calls went unanswered, according to IBM. As a result, businesses are investigating how to integrate AI into their processes so that they may speak with customers directly. AI, for instance, may provide clients with automated replies and FAQs, whereas human agents frequently become fatigued when managing activities that need many data. Additionally, AI can assist with data filtering, acquisition, analysis, search, answering repetitive inquiries, and mundane activities.

Benefits of AI in Customer Service

1. Manage Big Data Volumes

The next important thing in customer service is artificial intelligence (AI), which can address a common issue for businesses: the overwhelming amount of data. The customer service industry is being revolutionized by augmented intelligence technology, which will make it more effective, efficient, and profitable.

2. Shorten Customer Service Time

Most businesses need help responding to client inquiries, such as raising the number of agents to match the rise in consumer traffic. All consumer inquiries must be handled effectively and efficiently at the same time. Additionally, this response must occur quickly. For example, businesses with a high volume of one-off clients would prefer to wait five minutes on hold with a live person than twenty for an automated callback.

3. Identify Customer Needs and Expectations

Trying to satisfy customers' ever-higher expectations is one of the toughest challenges in customer service. It's never enough, even when you're doing a fantastic job.

Personalization is the solution. With AI, personalization is improved.

Personalization can be challenging. How do you understand what people require? How can you tell what they prefer? How can you know what they desire? You can better identify client wants and expectations by integrating AI into your customer service operation.

4. Provide prompt support

Most customer support software programs available today are created to offer reactive support, i.e., they assist clients while they are experiencing issues or problems. However, the most fantastic time to address a customer's issue is before it arises. AI is a potent tool for proactive problem-solving and support. AI allows you to:

◊ Determine the source of a problem by comparing current encounters and conversations with earlier ones.
◊ Recognize trends in client questions received via various sources.
◊ Cases should be automatically prioritized according to urgency and client problems.
◊ Send out preventative messages when a customer is dissatisfied or having a problem.

As artificial intelligence (AI) technology develops, it can suggest improvements to processes and procedures to make businesses function more efficiently and provide proactive support and opportunity identification. So, the next time your business requires customer support software, consider the advantages of giving proactive help using AI.

5. Be Flexible to Situational Change

Many businesses that use human resources for customer support must cope with many service requests and must, as a result, hire an increasing number of staff members.

Due to artificial intelligence (AI) and machine learning (ML), the customer service environment is evolving. Therefore, when a customer's behavior changes, AI can adjust.

- ◊ It can aid in locating fresh service gaps.
- ◊ It can generate a unified view of the customer experience across all channels and forecast when customers may leave.
- ◊ It can give the agent knowledge, insights into the consumer, and guidance on responding to various customer circumstances. In addition, concentrating on high-priority cases might lessen the workload of personnel.
- ◊ It can examine many facts to help you make better judgments.

Last but not least, in the upcoming years, AI will be applied not just to customer support systems but also in the retail and travel sectors, enabling businesses to amass more data on their clients and offer them better services.

6. Simpler Performance Monitoring

Performance monitoring and measurement are crucial in the workplace to determine how well your team works together. But occasionally, especially if you need to start using the correct tool or using one, it may be a laborious effort to make sure you're doing everything you can to boost your team's performance.

Many organizations have already realized that artificial intelligence (AI) can boost customer service. Customer experience must include excellent customer service (CX). It can ultimately make or ruin a corporation. You can use the AI platform's data, graphs, and metrics to evaluate your team's performance.

7. Identify Upcoming Trends

In the fashion sector, AI can be used to anticipate the trend of a well-known brand and the style of the associated fashion elements, like the Google News algorithm, but with a picture that can affect the fashion industry's trends instead of just text.

8. More time to concentrate on challenging issues

Most lesser activities may now be hand by autonomously by artificial intelligence (AI) systems, freeing workers' time to focus on more essential duties. For instance, Nara Logics uses AI to assist radiologists in reading CT scans and other diagnostic images. However, because these images frequently do not follow established sizes and are subject to human mistakes, they are incredibly challenging for humans to comprehend.

Deep learning is used by Precision, which Uber purchased in 2016, to assist warehouse workers in locating things in sizable fulfillment facilities. By utilizing AI to arrange photographs, Facebook frees up staff time to engage in more complex duties like maintaining the image collection across all of the social networking properties owned by Facebook, including Instagram and WhatsApp.

9. Customized Services and Products

By 2025, the International Data Corporation projects that the market for artificial intelligence will be worth $36.8 billion. Although artificial intelligence (AI) has made inroads into several sectors, including retail, healthcare, and financial services, the customer service sector has yet to see a similar level of adoption. On-demand, immediate support, as well as self-service, are made possible by AI in customer service.

AI may be used to track consumer complaints and queries without human input. This allows companies with extensive customer support teams to save costs and increase efficiency. In addition, many businesses can utilize AI to improve customer experiences by providing more individualized service to clients through live chat or voice assistants like Alexa and Siri.

Businesses that spend money on AI solutions stand to gain a lot. Since companies depend on product sales to expand economically, a 10% increase in sales volume would result in a 15% rise in profit.

10. Cut expenses

Almost all of the major IT companies use AI in some capacity to offer customer care. Companies are already cutting their cost of providing customer care by up to 80% by offering a "chatbot" or an automated manner. What about the clients, however? How does this benefit them?

First, there are no human operators, no standing in line forever, and, worst of all, no human errors. What if you could ask a question and instantly receive a response from a bot that could also learn from your interactions and form its own AI personality? You could never obtain that from any other human being on the planet!

In today's cutthroat business world, revenue growth is never guaranteed when new items are introduced daily. However, businesses will be able to remain competitive by using AI in customer service to keep their consumers satisfied and boost profitability.

How will AI help with customer service in the future?

Because it reflects customer engagement, the customer service sector has always been a crucial business component.

Since consumers can now contact brands globally and anytime, this sector is more crucial than ever. Therefore, customer service must adapt and adopt new procedures and technology to stay relevant. When we consider that more than 70% of individuals would only refer a brand to a friend if their interaction with it were positive, customer service's significance is highlighted.

Therefore, offering top-notch customer service should be every brand's primary objective. But what exactly does this consist of?

Today, a variety of factors influence customer service, including.

- ◊ Customer service using artificial intelligence (AI); personalization technology; performance management; quality assurance; and usability testing.
- ◊ Customer service encompasses more than just the internal division that addresses client complaints and questions. It is essential to many companies' brandings and significantly impacts how prospective customers view them. As a result, AI is now widely used in customer support.

Transportation

Over the past few hundred years, the transportation sector has witnessed numerous transformations and revolutions. We are now at a point where significant advancements in artificial intelligence are being made.

AI is capturing the attention of transportation executives worldwide through self-driving cars for excellent dependability, road condition monitoring for increased safety, or traffic flow analysis for greater efficiency. The tremendous potential of AI has tremendously been recognized by many in the transportation industry, and by 2026, it's expected that the global market will be worth $3,870,000,000.

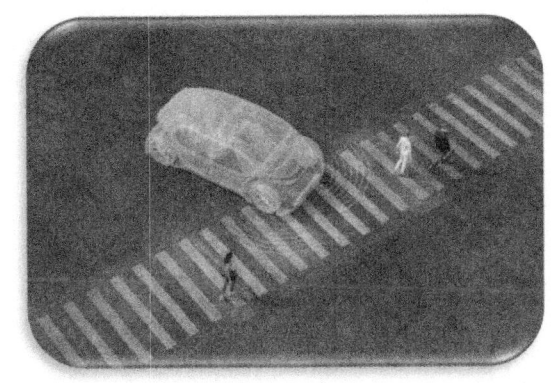

With innovative technologies like computer vision and machine learning, businesses can influence the future of transportation by enhancing passenger safety, lowering the number of accidents, and easing traffic congestion.

In transportation, deep learning and machine learning can also aid in developing "smart cities," as we have seen in Glasgow, where the technology is used to track trends in traffic density, parking violations, and vehicle dwell durations.

Autonomous Vehicles

Self-driving cars are not an original idea. General Motors first released it in 1939. However, corporations may now use computer vision techniques like object detection to create intelligent systems that can decode and grasp visual data, enabling a car to drive itself. This is only possible in the age of AI transportation.

The premise for creating the AI that powers self-driving cars is also simple: after being fed enormous amounts of pertinent data, the algorithm is trained to recognize specific objects and then conduct the appropriate actions, such as braking, turning, speeding up, slowing down, and so on.

What needs to be recognized by a model?

The presence of other cars, traffic signals, lane markings, road signs, pedestrians, and more. Autonomous vehicles employ cameras and sensors to gather and use data. The model must be regularly fed massive amounts to be trained and dependable. Naturally, there are still some difficulties. An algorithm must access vast amounts of pertinent data, and environmental factors like inclement weather and uneven terrain can complicate matters further. Other problems include dim lighting and the potential for an unidentified object to be discovered by a self-driving car while it is on the road.

Tesla comes to mind when most people think of self-driving cars. However, Tesla, Uber, Waymo, and Motional have been developing automated vehicles for years, always ahead of the curve.

Unlike other AI in transportation companies, Tesla's autonomous driving stack uses camera-equipped cars to capture video and image data without HD maps or lidars. However, this strategy is technically more difficult because the neural networks are trained solely on video input, making accuracy critical.

Traffic Monitoring (and Traffic Signs)

In only the US, there are hundreds of traffic lights. While it may seem straightforward to stop when a light turns red, the fact that in the US each year, about 1,000 people are killed needlessly by cars that run red lights makes the whole thing an extremely dangerous, deadly, and even intricate game.

It's a game with terrible results, too—passengers or drivers who didn't run a red light were responsible for nearly 50% of those fatalities.

The issue is that while the traffic signal system may be faultless in and of itself, drivers are sometimes faultless. Accidents arise when mistakes are made and when drivers occasionally run red lights.

With smart cities, autonomous vehicles can solve this awful situation and stop those deaths. As a result, automakers are making their self-driving cars' ability to deal with traffic signals their top priority.

An AI-based system can recognize green, amber, and red lights using computer vision models trained in various settings, such as dim lighting, bad weather, and occlusions.

In this way, a self-driving car's cameras first detect a traffic light before analyzing and processing the image, and if it finds that the light is red, the vehicle applies the brakes.

Detection of Pedestrians

How impressive would it be if a computer program could recognize and automatically locate pedestrians in pictures and videos? What if we could develop a model enabling autonomous vehicles to discern a pedestrian's purpose in real-time, for instance, if the pedestrian intended to cross the road?

A system like this would undoubtedly aid autonomous vehicles in avoiding hazardous circumstances, potentially significantly reducing the number of traffic accidents.

Because walkers can be incredibly unexpected in the setting of road traffic, pedestrian detection is a significant issue in computer vision and pattern recognition. Moreover, they are one of the biggest threats to the success of self-driving automobiles because they are so unpredictable.

The most important thing is that a system can correctly distinguish a human from another object and comprehend what a pedestrian will do next rather than only being able to recognize individual human traits like beards and noses.

Analysis of Traffic Flow

In addition to having an impact on road safety, traffic flow can have a positive or negative effect on a nation's economy. In addition to adding to global warming, traffic congestion wastes time and money, stresses out drivers and passengers, and costs money.

A nation's economy may develop more effectively with greater traffic flow, and the safety of its road users is significantly increased.

With this in mind, it should be no surprise that Artificial Intelligence is opening new possibilities for better traffic flow analysis using machine learning and computer vision. As a result, AI can assist in eliminating choke points and removing bottlenecks that are otherwise congesting our economy and our highways. For example, drones and camera-based traffic flow tracking and estimate are now viable due to computer vision improvements.

Monitoring of Road Conditions

According to estimates, pothole damage costs American drivers more than $3,000,000,000 annually, making it a severe problem.

However, for a long time, most road condition monitoring has been put in the hands of the public, whose "job" is to alert local councils about damaged roadways. Today, defection can be successfully detected by computer vision in transportation AI, and the surrounding infrastructure may be evaluated by searching for changes in the asphalt and concrete.

Using computer vision techniques, potholes may be identified, and the damage to the road can be shown so that the proper authorities can take action to improve road maintenance. In addition, algorithms collect and analyze visual data to create automatic crack detection and categorization systems. These will promote preventative maintenance and focused rehabilitation that doesn't involve humans.

In other words, it won't be the residents' job to report potholes and other road issues. Instead, AI systems will make real-time updates to enable quicker action. Again, this reduces waste and costs. The overall goal of Automated Pavement Distress (PD) detection is to increase road safety such that accidents are drastically decreased while also boosting the efficiency of road maintenance allocation.

Security

AI requires less human administration than many other security measures, which is a significant benefit for security. Therefore, adopting AI for essential use cases to support other goods makes sense. In addition, one can begin to weave together different jobs in an organized sequence as the models develop and users gain confidence in the system (much like with automation).

Modern security solutions work best for specific use cases, such as detecting and confidently eliminating phishing, spam, or opportunistic infection on endpoints. To get better over time, AI must be able to learn from these interactions by making observations and drawing logical conclusions.

Why is the security of artificial intelligence important?

Although AI security is the next step in cyber defense, is it necessary? It can take time to provide a clear answer to this issue. What is apparent is that traditional cybersecurity is becoming more challenging due to continual developments in malicious code and other threats. Almost 60% of enterprises today think that without artificial intelligence technologies, they would be unable to recognize essential dangers.

Think about the following elements:

◊ AI contributes to the reinforcement of cybersecurity workforce gaps.

Globally, the rate of digital change is accelerating. Sadly, the supply of knowledgeable, certified cybersecurity personnel must be kept up. Millions of cybersecurity positions go unfilled due to a talent gap that artificial intelligence can close. Using AI for security tools is a scalable option because they improve workers' workflows. Additionally, AI shortens the time it takes to recognize and prioritize risks, freeing critical resources. Workers may concentrate on more challenging jobs by automating easier, more challenging ones.

◊ AI encourages quicker danger detection.

It takes a long time to find dangers; single alert investigations might go on for days. Security technologies with AI capabilities can prioritize incidents, reducing the time needed for incident response.

◊ AI enables companies to prevent threat escalation.

Threat actors don't share certain firms' hesitation in adopting the most recent developments in digital security. According to Microsoft, "during the past year, threat actors have significantly improved in sophistication, utilizing strategies that make them tougher to recognize and endanger even the smartest targets." As a result, organizations are given the technologies they need by AI for security to keep up with this trend.

Human Resources

Coherent computing techniques and preprogrammed algorithms are used by artificial intelligence to make judgments in real-time. As a result, the field of human resources will be impacted by artificial intelligence.

When the human element of human resources is combined with the intelligence of technology, businesses can offer applicants and employees better conditions. HR AI will also promote the significance of delivering objectives more swiftly and effectively.

AI applications in HR

The hiring and training of new staff is a tiresome task for the human resources department. Artificial intelligence may assist human resources workers with their physical job in several ways.

◊ Recruiting & Talent Acquisition

Talent acquisition is essential for the HR department since adding skilled people will likely lead to the company's growth. AI is often used in HR when finding and hiring good people. AI cuts down on the time and effort needed to do these tedious tasks, like sifting through applications, managing databases, setting up interviews, and answering and solving questions from contestants.

So, the HR team can focus on more critical tasks, such as sourcing, managing employees, marketing recruitment, and other valuable lessons. It also makes the hiring process much shorter and saves time. In addition, selecting a candidate who largely satisfies the company's standards will be made more accessible with the help of AI-assisted recruitment. As a result, the screening process is easy, efficient, and fair.

Through chatbots, the candidates with the most potential are located and contacted. The newly hired employees are managed by these automated chatbots, which give them jobs and positions by their job profiles. It will first select the most qualified candidate who fits the job description. The top applicants will, after that, be scheduled for job interviews.

◊ Training of fresh recruits:

AI-based unified systems will teach new hires about business rules and knowledge on their first day on the job.

All necessary information, such as job profile information, corporate policies, work assignments, team member information, etc., will be sent to new employees via a mobile application or structured data on their laptops. This process is referred to as onboarding.

To increase the HR team's ability to recall and work effectively, onboarding is crucial. Candidates who experience a smooth and educational onboarding process are likelier to stick with the company over the long term. In addition, the AI for HR can answer all the questions potential candidates may ask, saving the personnel from having to do it manually.

Artificial intelligence allows HR procedures to be tailored to the workers' needs and associated tasks. Additionally, AI keeps track of the company's crucial contact information and other activities like validating legal documents.

◊ Recruits are being trained:

Employees can research and educate themselves on relevant jobs and requirements using AI development services. Giving them information about new software and technology in the field will also help them stay current. After looking at the papers and tests, the AI will automatically figure out what training the employee needs and give it to them.

Based on their work, description relevant will be given appropriate skill set information for better advancement. For example, AI-based HR technology could look at data and let the HR team know if an employee needs training. This intelligent method will improve workers' productivity and intelligence while helping them learn more swiftly and efficiently. In addition, they can train specific programs and teaching techniques so employees can learn independently and perform in line with business requirements.

◊ Improved employee experience:

Because there is much automation and a strong focus on the customer experience in the environment, employees can expect a positive and helpful time when they join the customized engagement. Consumer technology is shaping employee experiences, and employees are looking for options for how they want to be engaged and supported.

AI can be used throughout the employee lifecycle, from hiring and onboarding to providing HR services and planning a career path, to give each employee a personalized experience.

With personalized feedback forms and employee appreciation initiatives, human resources departments can now assess employee engagement and job satisfaction more precisely than ever. This is extremely helpful, given the importance of comprehending employees' general needs. However, there are numerous critical organizational advantages to possessing this understanding.

◊ Leadership:

Because AI will aid in developing trainees, it will improve the working practices of project managers and trainers in a firm. The AI will examine the structure of the leader's capabilities by asking questions of the members of their separate teams, and it will provide them with the abilities they need or adaptive traits.

Second, by examining the dashboard, managers may assess their performance and adapt their skill sets to the demands of the workplace.

Legal Services

The deployment of artificial intelligence (AI) computers, particularly by in-house lawyers, is causing a revolution in the legal profession and industry. This focuses on the numerous real-world applications of AI in legal departments and their advantages.

It is helpful to understand how businesses as a whole are adopting AI before determining the several ways legal departments might employ it. The apparent reason why firms like AI are worth highlighting for both is: Technology does not get hungry or need breaks when nature calls, nor does it get weary, sleep in, take sick days, or go on vacation. Instead, technology always continues developing new capabilities. That is a significant advantage for any business and its legal department.

E-discovery and AI

Most in-house attorneys are familiar with using AI for e-discovery (though I promise I will not make you read another article on e-discovery). In this case, the first application of AI was searching through megabytes of data for keywords. By doing this, a remarkable amount of time and money that would have been spent on attorneys to look for papers that might be pertinent was saved. Later, AI was used to connect email chains and remove duplicate documents, doing in minutes what would typically take days for humans to complete. And finally, going well beyond straightforward keyword searches, AI can now use predictive coding to search documents for context, concepts, and tone. Even internal compliance investigations employ predictive coding to sift through mountains of data quickly.

What more is AI capable of?

The use of AI for e-discovery is extensive, and its advantages in terms of time and cost are clear. But is that all in-house attorneys do? The quick response is no. The more extended response is undoubtedly "no." Legal AI has potential, and significant developments have already been made.

While many outside law firms are working on AI applications, in-house legal departments have the most potential to have a considerable influence. Internal legal departments are more motivated to discover cost-effective solutions than law firms, which find ways to provide services at a lower cost (i.e., the thumber of billable hours vs. quality of a billable hour). Considering this, the following is a summary of some of the disruptive and helpful things AI can already accomplish for in-house legal departments:

1. Reviews for due diligence.

Suppose you've participated in a due diligence review for a corporate transaction. In that case, you know that it typically entails a team of attorneys searching through documents (either in hard copy or electronically) in search of litigation concerns, significant contract provisions (such as change of control, MFN, termination, assignment, etc.), corporate, intellectual property, etc. It requires many people (typically outside counsel) and many hours or days to finish. AI-powered solutions can automate this procedure by looking for specific legal ideas and producing written reports about what was discovered.

2. Establish contracts

The "Holy Grail" for in-house attorneys who create contracts is the ability to create and use a format that complies with standard terms and conditions and requires (or permits) only minor alterations or customization. Form contracts let the business have a uniform set of agreements, save a ton of old ones that can draft contracts based on any criteria the legal department deems significant. The tool can also be configured such that clients can "self-serve," meaning they can log in, choose the kind of contract they need, add a few details, and the system will generate a ready-to-use standard form agreement. The legal department can decide how much involvement it wants in the production process, such as a quick evaluation of all contracts produced by the system (or at the slightest sign-off process), just seeing warranties of a specific type, or if the customer needs something nonstandard.

3. Management of contracts

A contract storage and management system—where contracts can be saved and managed by the agreement's provisions—is a real pain for every in-house lawyer. For instance, when must the renewal notice be sent out, and what is the termination date? Is there a clause that allows for price escalation? If so, when is this allowed, and what, if any, kind of notification is needed?

Traditionally, everything has been done by hand. Someone makes a spreadsheet and manually keeps track of everything or manually enters the data into a program that automatically handles the essential terms and dates. Except for early setup and fine-tuning, AI has advanced to the point where crucial information entry (terms, dates, and other information) can be completed by technology. The tools used to produce the contracts may also be used to manage contract management, including the signature procedure.

This results in an automated process from creation to storage. The effort required to review the current contracts and input that data into the new database is another obstacle to contemplating a contract management technology. AI can evaluate your whole database of contracts (from whichever sources are utilized to store contracts) and analyze and arrange those agreements in a way that would take a team of people months and months to do. Additionally, solutions can examine your whole contracts database, manage risk, and guarantee consistent monitoring and uniformity across your contracts.

4. Analysis of legal operations and spending

Most internal legal departments are switching to electronic invoicing systems. However, some still use paper bills. The e-billing system has a wealth of information, but regrettably, many in-house lawyers need help to extract it effectively. AI is resolving that issue by enabling analysis of the work completed, its alignment with other work conducted by the firm, its efficiency relative to work given by different firms contracted by the corporation, and its performance relative to the market. Think about having that knowledge when discussing billing rates with your law companies. Furthermore, there are operational solutions that may give you information and dashboards displaying the nature of the work entering legal, the personnel working on it, the progress made so far, and the risk profile of that work. Additionally, it can give case management capabilities and delegate the work to the appropriate lawyers (internal or external).

5. Analysis of litigation

    The public records of the U.S. judicial system include a staggering quantity of information. All relevant information, including court rulings, jury verdicts, and other essential documents, is readily available. Wouldn't it be wonderful to look through all that information and foresee how a case will turn out? Naturally, AI is already offering a solution in this case as well. Soon, it will be able to forecast how your case will turn out by comparing the facts of your case to those of other issues that have already been resolved by a court (or courts). What are our chances of winning a case? is a frequent query for in-house attorneys. Such a tool might offer some much-needed analytics for what a gut decision is frequently.

6. Legal investigation Legal research is another application.

    Most of the time, in-house attorneys either need to catch up on the research process because they need more time or resources to conduct a thorough job or pay a legal firm to have a first- or second-year attorney muddle through the issue. With the help of AI, you can ask about legal issues in simple terms and receive a response that incorporates research into rules, precedent, secondary sources, and more. Additionally, AI might be used as a FAQ service that can respond to your in-house clients' typical legal, HR, and compliance queries while being wise enough to know when to refer the question to an honest lawyer. The crucial point is that, in addition to time and money savings, the use of AI gives in-house counsel the one luxury that perpetually seems to be lacking: the luxury of leisure to reflect on the issue and offer the finest legal judgment and analysis.

Education and School

Artificial intelligence (AI) uses computers and other technologies to perform tasks by simulating human perception, decision-making, and other processes. In other words, AI describes how computers recognize intricate patterns and gain knowledge as they do so.

The nature of AI can be understood in a variety of ways. AI with rules-based and AI with machine learning-based assessment methods are two examples. The former generates a suggestion or a solution using decision-making rules. In this respect, it is the most basic form. An intelligent teaching system (ITS), which can give pupils detailed and targeted feedback, illustrates this technology.

AI enhances student-specific learning plans and curricula, promotes tutoring by assisting students in honing their abilities and fortifying their weak areas, fosters rapid communication between instructors and students, and enhances accessibility to learning for everyone around the around-the-clock. In addition, educators can use AI to automate tasks, including administrative labor, learning pattern analysis, paper grading, answering general questions, and more. The following are eight applications of AI in education.

1. **Designing courses**

Creating instructional materials is a significant time and financial commitment for the central department. The application of AI streamlines the process of making courses, accelerating it and cutting costs. AI course creation software can assist in producing interactive content with ease, whether you are working from scratch or using prepared templates. To efficiently generate the best training materials, your team can collaborate with you via in-app feedback from reviewers and co-authors.

AI makes course development easier and faster. AI provides teachers with a clear image of the classes and subjects that need reevaluation by evaluating student learning history and ability. Teachers modify their courses by assessing students' unique needs to fill common knowledge gaps. As a result, educators can create the most effective learning plans for every student.

2. **Providing individualized education**

A critical trend in education is personalization. Based on their tastes and experiences, AI offers pupils a personalized learning strategy. AI can adjust to students' knowledge levels, intended goals, and learning rates to help them get the most out of their education. Additionally, AI-powered programs may evaluate a student's academic record, identify areas for development, and suggest courses, providing numerous chances for individualized instruction.

3. **Facilitating open access**

AI dismantles the barriers between traditional grade levels and school systems. Students with visual or hearing impairments and those who speak other languages can now access courses worldwide thanks to AI tools. For example, a PowerPoint plugin like Presentation Translator offers real-time subtitles for everything the teacher says for students who need to study at distinct levels, want to learn subjects not provided at their school, or are absent.

4. **Identifying course improvement areas**

Teachers can only sometimes be aware of the gaps in their lectures and teaching materials, which might need clarification on specific concepts. AI offers a remedy for this problem. Coursera is already using this, for example. When several students submit incorrect responses to their homework assignments, the system notifies the professor and provides upcoming students with personalized messages that offer pointers for the correct answer.

This program ensures students construct a similar conceptual foundation and fill in the course explanation gaps. In addition, students receive quick feedback to aid their understanding of subjects rather than waiting for the teacher's reply.

5. **Automating work**

Teachers frequently have many on their plates, including managing courses and other administrative and organizational duties. They handle instructional materials, organize lecture resources and materials, grade tests, assess assignments, complete necessary paperwork, create progress reports, and more.

As a result, they could get overworked from devoting too much time to things other than teaching. Instead, educators can automate manual tasks using automation tools and solutions, freeing more time to educate students in critical competencies.

6. **Assisting with tutoring**

Intelligent tutoring programs and systems, such as AI chatbot tutors, are made to manage individualized feedback and educational recommendations. But since they need more sophistication to impart knowledge in the same manner as humans, they cannot take the position of teachers. Nevertheless, they are helpful when teachers are unavailable for subjects that can be taught and evaluated online.

Using AI, E-learning systems may effectively teach geography, languages, circuits, computer programming, medical diagnostics, physics, mathematics, chemistry, genetics, and other subjects. They are prepared to consider comprehension, engagement, and grading measures. AI technologies help students improve their weak areas and hone their talents outside the classroom.

7. Supporting online education

Group educational activities, student counseling, and immersive learning experiences can all be facilitated in a virtual learning environment. With the help of VR technologies, students can link their laptops or mobile devices directly to the content. With VR headsets, kids with ADHD and ADD can reduce interruptions and lengthen their attention spans. In addition, through interactive simulations, students can coach others in soft skills, self-improvement, and life skills.

8. Making intelligent content

Brilliant content, which creates tailored settings for learning organizations based on goals and tactics, can include digital guides, textbooks, videos, instructional snippets, and AI. By identifying the areas where AI solutions contribute, it will be possible to implement personalization in the education sector, a potential global trend. For instance, a school can create a learning environment based on augmented reality or virtual reality (AR/VR) and web-based classes to go along with it.

Professional sport coaching

Our favorite sporting activities are quickly altering due to artificial intelligence (AI). With applications ranging from revealing the secrets to athletic success to changing coaching strategies, preventing injuries, and even allowing spectators to get a behind-the-scenes look at their favorite sports stars' performances, the $1.6 billion AI in the sports sector is currently all the rage.

But how did we quickly transition from stopwatches and chalkboards to machine learning and prediction algorithms? Programmers worked hard creating algorithms to include sports in the new computing generation as technology advanced, and processing power soared. When combined with cutting-edge technology like wearables and athlete tracking systems, AI can transform an essential piece of equipment into a multipurpose tool. One that can accurately forecast performance gains and losses and evaluate data in real time.

Sports AI's Top Advantages

AI in sports represents a significant advancement in quantifying and comprehending the vast volumes of data at our disposal. We can finally dig into minute detail and use them to refine and perfect our performances thanks to artificial intelligence's (AI) capacity to process and learn athletic data at great rates and with outstanding precision.

◊ Both Coaches and Athletes

Athlete tracking systems with AI-powered tailored training can do more than monitor performance on the field. They can also maintain tabs on everything going on off of it. For example, wearables and other technology may detect anything from stress levels to travel distances, and AI can enhance off-season training plans and recovery efficiency. This makes it easier for physicians, physical therapists, coaches, and athletes to control their workloads. As a result, they can create specialized training plans that maximize exercise benefits and lower or even eliminate the chance of injury.

- ◊ Enhanced group analytics

Today, coaches may use AI to make data-driven, unbiased judgments on the performance of individuals, teams, and even skill levels. Most trainers would miss items that AI can identify while providing them with accurate, up-to-date information. Real-time and historical analytics, including those of athletes in competition

Coaches and athletes can now monitor their performance in real time and make judgments immediately rather than waiting for the game's outcome. This allows for real-time adjustments to plays and strategy, tracking, and quick-response tactics from the enemy.

For both supporters and other people

- ◊ Stronger adherence and support

Because we feel like we're a part of their journey, we tend to love our sports heroes more when we have a deeper understanding of their careers. AI breakthroughs in sports give viewers—both existing and prospective—a greater understanding of athletic performances, trends, injury updates, and overall shape, encouraging a more devoted audience.

- ◊ Improved Predictability

The key strength of AI is its capacity to analyze enormous amounts of data, apply algorithms, and make impressively accurate predictions about what's most likely to occur next. The most likely result of a race, match, or competition can be predicted by AI, even though it cannot predict the future. This adds flavor to the fantasy league and sports betting scenes and gives a more thrilling overall experience.

These are only a few of the fantastic advantages AI gives sports, and the development is already resulting in enormous improvements in athlete capabilities and training results. For athletes, their coaches, and the fans alike, this results in tremendous success on the field and a higher return on investment.

What Role Does AI Play in the Sports Sector?

◊ AI in coaching

For professional, collegiate, and amateur coaches, AI is quite helpful. They can use it to make crucial strategic choices regarding their teams or particular players that are supported by indisputable statistics. AI-connected cameras, sensors, and trackers also make it possible to examine data before, during, and after a game, allowing coaches to decide what is best for their players. AI helps coaches devise strategies and tactics based on information gathered during games or even throughout an entire season.

◊ Artificial intelligence for improving athletic performance

The secret to raising performance is training. Players may now use technologies like HomeCourt, which uses computer vision and machine learning to assess abilities and give detailed feedback, thanks to the most current developments in sports AI. Athletes can use this to pinpoint their areas of improvement, concentrate on them throughout training, and track their growth. Simple but powerful.

◊ AI for sports analytics and outcome forecasting

When it comes to sports analytics, AI is unbeatable. AI in sports analytics may be used practically differently thanks to its powerful learning capabilities and advanced programming. Analyzing an athlete's performance is crucial, but understanding training results and growth is frequently essential for success. Many software programs available may be used to analyze sports performance. For instance, Svexa, a platform for tracking and analyzing athlete movement, creates individualized exercise and training suggestions using molecular profiling and a comprehensive grasp of technology. The NFL's scouting program employs Sparta Science, another well-liked choice, to evaluate and identify top college players by monitoring each applicant's real-world behavior.

Match prediction: We've always wondered if artificial intelligence can foretell sporting outcomes. Well, not quite yet, but it can come close. Because of the unpredictable nature of sports, there will inevitably be upsets, but AI is already proficient at foreseeing those. ML models can frequently forecast the outcome as the activity occurs on the field when a wealth of athletic data is available. For instance, during the IPL in cricket, students used AI to correctly predict a match's result while it was still going on! This model illustrated how teams could utilize AI to alter their play throughout a game to increase their odds of winning.

◊ Computerized Sports Journalism

AI sports are most suited for sports journalism. Automated reporting is gaining popularity since many statistics and facts are available, and many teams compete daily. In addition, journalists may now cover a much more comprehensive range of sports, leagues, and events than they previously could because of pre-defined templates, writing styles, and sophisticated prediction models.

◊ Stories based on data

With natural language production, tools like Wordsmith can now take actual data or measurements and turn them into narratives. The AP has expanded its reporting capabilities to cover 13 leagues and 14 MLB-affiliated teams, but sports media is just starting to take advantage of this new power.

- ◊ AI in sports enables journalists to add more data to their articles.

Match monitoring AI bots may now follow games in progress in real-time, providing live updates on significant developments, results, and statistics. Often, fans are shocked to realize that the reporter is an AI-powered computer that can accurately capture the enthusiasm and emotion of the game as it is happening.

- ◊ Quicker and Less Expensive

Sports media organizations like AP's sports division fast realize how much more affordable and competent an AI-powered reporter is than a human reporter. Sports journalism supported by AI is becoming quicker, less prejudiced, and more accurate than ever because of the ability to track various events and use structured data to produce fascinating content.

In sports reporting in some of the world's largest sports, AI solutions are becoming increasingly popular. However, journalists need help to keep up as live AI already manages live reporting sports like tennis, soccer, baseball, and basketball. Automated Insights and Narrative Science, two of the top natural language generation tech businesses in the US, began as projects to produce game summaries automatically.

- ◊ AI in streaming and broadcasting

AI in broadcasting and streaming services plays a crucial part in understanding consumers, providing them precisely what they want, and raising ratings as the streaming business grows. The same holds for streaming sports. Around 30% of sports fans already watch live sports material on mobile devices, and AI is helping to make highlights more interactive, accessible, and engaging.

◊ Utilizing current technology

Because the hardware is currently available, streaming is ideal for AI sports prospects. Due to its capabilities, AI sports streaming can automate existing video streaming and broadcasting systems. In addition, AI in sports enables us to develop sophisticated, scalable, and reliable networking solutions that work to customer requirements.

Retail

Profit and productivity must be prioritized in retail enterprises if they want to compete in the current global market. To achieve success and keep a lead over competitors, quick and effective action is needed. Artificial intelligence (AI) can enhance retail operations by boosting revenue and streamlining administrative procedures. By 2028, the value of AI services in the retail industry is expected to rise from $5 billion to more than $31 billion.

AI paves the way for companies to adopt "smart" staffing and replenishment choices that save labor and supply costs, assist in avoiding out-of-stock situations, and boost sales. Retail positions will change because of AI, improving corporate efficiency. Retail firms are more interested in learning how artificial intelligence changes the sector as technology develops. Here are a few of the industry's most important AI applications:

◊ **Automation**

Many tasks formerly completed by people are now routinely automated, thanks to artificial intelligence. As a result, employees may devote more time to providing excellent customer service and less time to tedious activities. Overall, this procedure boosts productivity and enhances the clientele's experience.

Computers have enabled enterprises in the retail sector to handle increasingly complex jobs, like resolving client issues. These developments lead to more significant sales, improved production, overall profit, and favorable environmental effects.

◊ **Loss avoidance**

Self-checkout innovation is being sparked by AI technology, which provides a safe scanning process and aids in reducing stealing. It can operate independently of human intervention, allowing customers greater control over purchasing. In addition, AI authentication will be employed in the new system to log information about shady shoplifters.

◊ **Consistency**

The potential for artificial intelligence to significantly increase the sustainability of retail operations. AI forecasting technologies help companies become carbon neutral by tracking emissions and encouraging recycling. Artificial intelligence has several benefits, including reducing the environmental impact of travel to physical stores and the amount of garbage dumped in landfills.

◊ **Reducing expenses**

Artificial intelligence may help retail companies organize and streamline their personnel, allowing them to make data-driven decisions. In addition, AI is expected to automate repetitive operations and improve more challenging work, like delivering, tracking, and scheduling. All these innovations can simplify and enhance workers' tasks significantly.

◊ **Supply chain improvement**

Artificial intelligence software can analyze consumer purchasing history and alarm when the stock of top-selling goods is dangerously low. For retailers, keeping their inventory well-stocked is crucial. As well as identifying seasonal item trends and forecasting peak demand periods for certain things, AI can offer insights into the temporal patterns of consumer demand.

Conclusion: The Future of AI and Generative AI

Mendelson believes that "generative adversarial networks" (GAN), which allow computer algorithms to create rather than assess by pitting two nets against each other, and "reinforcement" learning, which deals in rewards and punishments rather than labeled data, are two of the most fascinating areas of AI research and experimentation that will have implications in the next future. This is shown by Google DeepMind's Alpha Go Zero's Go prowess. The former is indicated by making one-of-a-kind visuals or sounds based on learning about subjects, such as renowned persons or a specific musical style.

AI can have a far-reaching impact on environmental challenges such as sustainability, climate change, and pollution. For example, cities will ideally become less crowded, less polluting, and more habitable as better sensors are deployed.

"Once you foresee something, you may dictate certain laws and processes," says Nahrstedt. For example, car flow might be enhanced by installing sensors on vehicles that offer data about traffic conditions and identify potential problems. This is far from over, she insists. It is still in its infancy. However, it will have a significant impact later.

Businesses are beginning to employ generative AI for various activities such as marketing, customer service, sales, learning, and client engagements, and it is fast becoming more widely used. For example, AI can create complex advertising strategies, pitch materials, and product concepts to improve conversion rates and money.

Companies that employ generative AI are seeing tremendous success in venture capital, with many raising large amounts and attaining high valuations. For example, hugging Face raised $100 million at a $2 billion valuation, Stability AI got $101 million at a $1 billion valuation, and Jasper, a creative assistant, just received $125 million at a $1.5 billion valuation, according to TechCrunch. In addition, TechCrunch claimed that Inflection AI raised $225 million at a post-money valuation of $1 billion. These accomplishments contrast with OpenAI, which received over $1 billion in funding from Microsoft in 2019 and was valued at $25 billion.

AI holds the key to a beautiful future in which we can all make better decisions with the assistance of data and technologies that grasp our reality. Future computers will understand why switches must be turned on and how to do it. They could even ask whether we'll need controls in the future.

AI can fundamentally alter how business is conducted, although it cannot resolve all of your organization's issues. Every industry is impacted, from banking to manufacturing, and productivity levels are at an all-time high. Additional applications will develop as more industries embrace and test this technology. Compared to the emergence of computing devices, AI will bring about considerably broader and more profound change. It will change how we do business, get diagnoses and treatments, and drive cars. It has already impacted computer vision, financial modeling, industrial processes, and medical imaging.

Printed in Great Britain
by Amazon